Using American Law Books

Second Edition

Alfred J. Lewis

University of California—Davis

**KENDALL/HUNT
PUBLISHING COMPANY**
Dubuque, Iowa

*Dedicated
to my wife Theresa
and my children Christopher, Josette, and Liza.*

Contents

Table of Illustrations

Table of Step by Step Instructions

Table of Correct Citation Forms

Foreword to the Student

In my early days in law school I had several moments in the law library where the crush of all those thousands of strange, dry, technical, unpleasant, and *thick* law books became overwhelming. I had heard vague references to "citators," "digests," "looseleaf services," "reporters," "*Corpus Juris Secundum,*" and dozens of other oddities, and wondered how could there be so many books on law.

Fortunately, I have since learned that all of this literature is not as complex as it first seems. If you concentrate on the fundamentals and see the overall patterns, you can obtain a working acquaintance with these materials in a short time. A really thorough knowledge of law books will only come with repeated use. There is nothing in this work that is difficult to understand, just difficult to remember a week later.

Do not plow through the book sentence by sentence. Read through each chapter to get the essential ideas first. **Ignore the footnotes for at least the first reading.** Extensive footnoting has been used so that you will not be burdened with too much detail at once. This permits the notation of peripheral details at the point where they are relevant.

Do at least some of your reading of this manual while in a law library. Look at the actual books on the shelves. Legal research is a practical skill that employs concrete objects. It is like learning to drive a car: you have to get your hands on the subject matter.

A study of American legal literature can be an interesting introduction to the fundamental structure and philosophy of our legal system. Admittedly, for those of you who are going to be lawyers, you may find that this practical subject lacks the color of Criminal Law, the grand themes of Constitutional Law, or the big bucks aura of

Taxation and Corporation Law. But it is part of a lawyer's basic lifetime skills; it is the one skill you can sell to a law firm or government agency over the summer or when you first get out of law school. You cannot tell them that you can interview their important clients, or do their trial work, or do most of the other things a lawyer does. But you can say that you can do their research—if you know your way around a law library, that is.

A. J. L.

Preface

Using American Law Books is intended as an introductory classroom textbook on legal bibliography and research techniques. It is suitable for first year law school courses in legal research, paralegal programs, undergraduate law related courses, and library science classes in legal bibliography. My experience in teaching law and non-law students is that they all bring nearly the same *tabula rasa* to class. It is a beginner's manual, and I think one should observe a clear distinction in style and content between a beginner's manual and a reference work on this subject. The latter is for the experienced legal researcher who occasionally needs to refer to detailed descriptions of the content, structure, and background of all law books.

It is a common mistake to overwhelm the beginner with too much detail while failing to adequately stress the essentials. Students should leave the course with a *working knowledge* of all the major categories of law books. They should be able to find a federal regulation, a state court rule, a sample pleading, a U.S. treaty, a recent state statute, and so forth. All we can do is to give them a framework on which to build. Much of the detail will have to be learned through experience.

With these thoughts in mind, I have tried to provide more than just another catalog of law book descriptions. Step-by-step instructions have been provided for the use of all the more complex tools. Beginners usually appreciate this guidance. In most chapters I have tried to go from the general to the specific. In annotated codes, for instance, it is important that students understand the overall structure of annotated codes and especially their relationship to session laws, before dealing with specific matters of numbering, supplementation, competing sets, and so on. It is so easy to forget the ignorance and misconceptions that the novice brings to this subject.

Patterns of publication (for example, in case reporting—the official/ unofficial and state/federal parallels) have also been brought to the student's attention.

It is paramount, in teaching this material, to keep the student constantly oriented. Otherwise, it all turns into a confusing array of pamphlets, sections, advance sheets, blue books, codes, supplements, digests, citations, headnotes, pocket parts, parallel tables, annotations, indexes, committee reports, registers, forms for motions, looseleaf services, and on and on and on. Throughout this work I have attempted to distinguish the essential from the less essential. Important, but less essential details have been relegated to footnotes. *The student should initially read through each chapter one or more times, ignoring the notes.* He or she will then be in a position to fit in some of the finer points.

To also aid in orientation, and to touch base with reality, the student is constantly encouraged in the text to look at the actual books in a law library while reading the manual. Sample pages have been reproduced in the text but a sample page is only a small part of the entire context. Typically, the full context is seeing a certain page, in a certain supplement, to a certain volume, in a certain multivolume set, which sits on the shelves of a certain law library. It is easy to teach these materials to a few people in a law library; it is difficult to do it in a classroom.

I have provided the correct citation form as soon as a new source is introduced. The citation samples are in accordance with the rules of the thirteenth edition of the "Harvard Blue Book."

As a final aid to orientation, all of the law books covered have been categorized under the headings of cases, codes, or commentaries. This is another device to help the student to organize these materials in his memory. It is also the framework that most closely corresponds with how American lawyers look at their literature: Are there any cases on point? Is there a statute (or regulation)? Is there a law review article, book, or service on the subject?

A **Problems Supplement** is available containing 275 short answer drills for use in a law library. An **Instructor's Manual** is also available with the answers and occasional commentaries and teaching hints. Both are keyed to the text.

Acknowledgments

I would like to thank Professors Jean Love and Friedrich Juenger of the University of California at Davis School of Law for their advice and encouragement. Jean Love was especially helpful in the early drafts of the 1976 edition.

I owe a special debt to Professor John W. Truslow of Georgia State University for his informed and insightful review of the manuscript for the 1983 edition and for prodding my thinking about the basic organization of legal materials.

John E. Pickron, Librarian and Associate Professor of Law at the University of Hawaii School of Law performed the extraordinary favor of reading the current manuscript. A number of improvements are attributable to his conscientious and informed attention.

Thanks are also due to law librarians Silvia Gonzalez of the University of California at Davis and Tom Reynolds of the University of California at Berkeley and, finally, to Dolores Loiseaux for her accurate typing and cheerful patience with difficult copy.

Introductory Matters

Outline

Introductory Matters

I. History and Organization of Law Books

A. The Accessibility of American Law

There is no substantial body of literature in the world that is as accessible as American law. There are literally millions of appellate opinions, court rules, constitutions, statutes, charters, ordinances, treaties, executive orders, proclamations, and administrative regulations—coming from the three branches of government at the local, state, and national levels, and from fifty-one jurisdictions—that constitute that enormous body of laws enacted during our two hundred years of sovereign history. Yet, despite the enormity and complexity of this documentation, you can enter any one of the many large law libraries in the United States and expect to find any one of these laws.

All of this law is accessible for two reasons. First, it is elementary that if *Ignorantia juris non excusat,* then the government must make some effort to inform its citizenry. Second, the great size and wealth of this country, with its large amount of legal business, has created a market which private publishers have entered with sophisticated research tools.

B. The Beginnings of Legal Publishing

Many of the current types of law books have a long history. Back in the reign of Edward I (1272–1307) some people sat in on trials and recorded what happened and what was said. These "recorders" may have been neophyte lawyers trying to learn the business. The accounts were later collected in a series called the *Year Books.* From that time, in an unbroken line to the present day, law reporting has continued in England, the United States, and the other common law countries.

It is presumed that it was an Englishman named Statham who first took it upon himself to produce a subject key to all of these cases that were accumulating in the "law reports" of the fourteenth and fifteenth centuries. In 1490 his *Abridgment of the Year Books* was published. That abridgment was the forerunner of today's legal digests.

During the reign of Edward III (1327–1377) the *Natura Brevium* and the *Novae Narrationes* were published. These books collected the writs and provided commentaries and notes from cases in the *Year Books*. They are the ancestors of the modern pleading and practice sets.

Blackstone's monumental *Commentaries on the Laws of England* (1765–69) was the last in a line of scholarly, yet practical, encyclopedic treatises on the common law. Its ancestors were the works of Glanvil, Bracton, Littleton, and Coke. In modern times, the tradition has been carried on in the United States by Prosser on Torts, Corbin on Contracts, Bogert on Trusts, and others. Today, the law is too broad for one man to encompass.[1] It is interesting that Blackstone went through more editions and was more important to the American bar than to the English bar. During our developmental years, when we had no native legal text books and few law books of any kind, Blackstone was often the beginning and end of an American lawyer's library—and education.

Today, it is the "continuing education of the bar," Matthew Bender, West, or one of the other publishers that is producing these encyclopedias, form books, and practical manuals for busy lawyers.

C. Order Out of Chaos: Cases, Codes, and Commentaries

The first time you enter a large law library, you may feel overwhelmed by the great number and variety of books you find there. How could there be so many books on just *law*? However, if you will stop and recall what you already know about our federal system and its many law-making units and then apply your common sense to the problem of how one would go about making all of that law accessible—you will be able to account for most of those books you see in a law library. There is far less mystery in law and law books than most people believe; 95% of it is common sense and logic.

First of all, you have to remind yourself that all three branches of our government are making law. Sometimes we tend to think only in terms of the legislative branch passing laws each year. But, in our common law system, courts are also making laws. When an appellate court reviews a trial court judgement, it is also setting a precedent and these precedents are published—that is what we mean by "cases." The executive branch is also making laws. Federal agencies are issuing thousands of regulations each year. The President is making treaties, and issuing proclamations, and executive orders. These are all "laws" and they all get published.

---

1. Bernard Witkin of California is, undoubtedly, the last to try. See his: *Summary of California Law, California Crimes, California Evidence,* and *California Procedure.*

Next, you have to remind yourself that laws are also coming from every level in our federal system. Thousands of city councils, county boards of supervisors, and the like are enacting ordinances—and law libraries collect these, at least locally. State governments are also making and publishing laws. State courts are deciding cases, state legislatures are enacting statutes, and state agencies are issuing regulations. One reason we have so many books is that there are fifty-one jurisdictions in the United States.

So, we have the published text of laws coming from all these sources sitting in law libraries. Our next question is how accessible is all this law? So far we have just been talking about the primary sources of law: books that contain the text of court opinions, legislative enactments, etc. The difficulty with these primary sources is their chronological arrangement. For example, there are literally tens of thousands of cases going back hundreds of years that are of interest to American lawyers. Legislation also piles up year after year. Earlier laws have been amended or repealed by later laws. Obviously you need law books that will give you subject access to the law in force. Many of the books in law libraries fall into this category. With legislation, for instance, all of the acts of a state that are still in force are arranged by subject and printed in statutory "codes."

Finally, as you might expect, with the complexity and ever changing nature of law, there is a need for works that explain, analyze, predict, criticize, and otherwise "comment" on the law; therefore, law libraries are filled with legal periodicals, textbooks, manuals, treatises, encyclopedias, and other "commentaries."

In this work, all these law books have been organized under three general headings: **cases, codes** and **commentaries.** In the typical legal research problem an American lawyer will ask himself or herself: Are there any cases on point? Should I check the statutory (or regulatory) codes? Should I read an article in a law review or a chapter in a treatise first?

In addition to knowing the categories of law books, there is one simple trick you should learn in order to discover the contents of many books—forget about the title on the cover, read the title page. Law books typically specify their contents and scope with a short, accurate statement on the title page. For example, the several hundred volume set of books called *Federal Supplement* might mean nothing to you until you read the statement on the title page that says: "Cases Argued and Determined in the United States District Courts. . . ."

II. Special Characteristics of Law Books

A. They are Designed for Lawyers, Not for Scholars

A social scientist will turn to a law library to find the status of legalized abortion in the fifty states. A lawyer will turn to a law library to find out if the Madison Joint Unified School District was liable when one of its temporary employees struck and damaged a stolen vehicle, at night, during a storm that blew down the stop sign, at an intersection in a neighboring state, when the employee was drunk, and was using the school bus for his own purposes and without authority. The lawyer's research might take a couple of hours. The social scientist might spend a year at his task. (It surprises many people to learn that there is no *single* index to *all* the state laws.) Law books are practical tools designed to answer those very specific questions arising from that phenomenon which is the foundation of all law: a particular controversy between individuals and/or organizations. Law is also jurisdictional. Its books are not designed to answer general questions.

B. Legal Supplementation

Since laws change constantly, law books must be constructed to accommodate frequent supplementation. A strict rule of legal research is: always update! Check the dates of publication or coverage of any book you are using.

One method of supplementation peculiar to law books is the "pocket part." A pocket part is a paperbound pamphlet that inserts into a pocket on the inside back cover of the book it supplements. Other devices include pamphlets shelved after the volume or set they supplement, replacement volumes, and replacement pages in looseleaf services.

C. Citation to Authorities

1. Citation Form

You will not use legal commentaries for long before noticing that legal writing is heavily annotated. Two sentences cannot be put together without citing authority (cases, statutes, etc.). This makes sense because no one wants to make decisions that affect life, liberty and property based merely on someone's word as to their legal effect.

Unlike many other annotated writings, in law, people frequently look up these citations. In fact, they may be more interested in the citations than the text. Rules of citation form, therefore, are critical. The most widely recognized compilation of these rules is *A Uniform System of Citation,* published by the Harvard Law Review Association. It is popularly known as the "Harvard Blue Book." Throughout this manual, the correct citation form has been indicated after each type of law book discussed. These sample citations are based on the "Blue Book."

2. Binding and Persuasive Authority

Binding authorities are those laws (generally referring to court opinions) that are controlling in a certain situation. For example, if a person is being tried in Texas for an alleged criminal act under the Texas Penal Code, his or her attorney will want to cite favorable Texas statutes and appellate court decisions, because the trial judge would be bound by these authorities.

There are other situations, however, where an attorney may want to cite persuasive authority. One is where there are no state statutes or cases on point and another is where the attorney is arguing to the highest appellate bench and is seeking a change in the state's case law. Such persuasive authorities could include decisions from other state courts, scholarly commentary from law reviews or treatises, the opinions of the state attorney general, or even other state statutes in special situations.

3. Holding and Dictum

Holding and dictum refer to the authority of various statements in appellate court opinions. An appellate bench not only decides to affirm, reverse or modify the lower court's decision, but also writes an "opinion" that sets forth an analysis of the issues in the case and explains the reasons for the decision. It is from a reading of the import of these opinions that holdings are determined. These holdings then become precedents (legal rules) for similar, subsequent cases.

For example, the Supreme Court of the United States, in *Brown v. Board of Education of Topeka,* 347 U.S. 483 (1954), reversed certain federal district court decisions and ruled that the racially segregated schools in specified districts in Kansas, South Carolina, Virginia, and Delaware were in violation of the equal protection clause of the Fourteenth Amendment. In one sense, the court was simply handing down a final adjudication on some specific controversies between individuals and certain school districts. As we all know, however, this case is precedent for the *rule of law* that any system of school segregation based solely on race is in violation of the equal protection laws of the Fourteenth Amendment. We also know that this holding extends to situations where the facilities are equal, because the court accepted it as fact that the Kansas facilities were equal.

Not everything the Court said was law, however. During the course of the opinion, Chief Justice Warren discussed the historical background for the adoption of the Fourteenth Amendment and made several statements to the effect that these historical sources were inconclusive on the question of what the drafters and ratifiers of the amendment intended it to mean in terms of public education. If you studied the opinion carefully, you would realize that these statements are dicta. The full expression for this concept is *obiter dicta* which means incidental words. As such, one cannot cite the *Brown* case as holding that you cannot use historical sources to determine the intent of the framers of the Fourteenth Amendment.

III. Law Libraries

There are several hundred law school or county law libraries in the United States which students and the general public may use. This is especially true if they are publicly supported. Law libraries serving particular courts, government departments, or other specialized clientele and libraries supported by bar association dues are not available to the public. In any case, you will be much more welcome if you know your way around law books. One thing you should be aware of is that most publications in law libraries are noncirculating. A legal collection is like one big "reference room." Most books have to be used within the building. You simply cannot permit someone to check out a volume of the United States Supreme Court decisions for two weeks. Of course, photocopiers have made it much easier to live with this rule.

As for you law students—spend some time in your law library. Study there, look things up, walk around! Pull down a volume of *Martindale-Hubbell*. It is much easier and less embarrassing to learn your way around a law library while in law school, rather than after. You can absorb much by simply seeing those books on the shelves every day.

SECTION

1

Cases

Section Outline

The Common Law System; How the Courts Make Law

I. Origins—England

There are two major legal regimes in the western world: the civil law system and the common law system.[2] Civil law developed from Roman law. It is based on the assumption that the legislature is the exclusive lawmaking branch of government. The legal codes of the civil law countries of Europe and other areas (notably Japan) are designed to cover the general principles of law. There is also great reliance on scholarly writings as sources of meaning of the law. In England, things happened differently . . .

In the late Middle Ages, when English law began its development in relative isolation from continental influences and without a strong Roman legacy, the practice arose of writing down accounts of the procedure and the reasoning applied at court trials. As noted earlier, these sketchy accounts may have initially been the private notes of fledgling lawyers trying to learn the mysteries of the law. As the reports of these cases gradually formalized, they came to be cited as precedent when similar cases arose.

And so, from a "time whereof the memory of man runneth not to the contrary,"[3] England has been developing a great body of law through this process of recording and following precedents. The technical name for the rule that drives this process is *stare decisis* (to stand by the decisions). The name for this body of law is the common law.

2. Other, non-western systems, except Socialist Law, generally have a religious origin and include: Jewish Law, Moslem Law, Hindu Law, Canon Law, and many primitive tribal and customary systems.

3. W. Blackstone, Commentaries, Book I, Intro. §3 (1765–69)

II. The United States

Because of our early history, we have inherited the common law and have continued its development to meet the situation in the United States. Most states have a statute that incorporates the "common law of England, so far as it is not repugnant to or inconsistent with the Constitution of the United States, or the Constitution of laws of this State. . . ."

According to the simplified view of our government, the legislative branch makes the law, the executive branch executes the law and the judicial branch applies the law. Of course, in fact, the courts *make* a great deal of law. This lawmaking occurs in three areas:

(1) Continuing the development of the common law.

(2) Interpreting statutes.

(3) Determining the constitutionality of government actions.

You do not have to be studying subjects like contracts or torts for very long before you realize that almost all of that law has been developed by the courts. But, the courts have another important lawmaking role in interpreting legislation. Statutes are often couched in such general language that their effect on the regulated activity cannot be determined until the courts apply the language to actual controversies. For example, the Sherman Antitrust Act of 1890 only initiated governmental control of monopoly. A complex legal specialty has arisen out of judicial interpretation of such statutory phrases as "restraint of trade or commerce," and "intrastate transactions." The courts' power to *interpret* legislation has always been construed liberally. In fact, they *make* a great deal of law in the process.

The last of the major functions of the courts is to determine if the law-making activities of the government are in accordance with the Constitution. Again, as with interpreting legislation, the courts create much law while applying the language of constitutional provisions. The United States Supreme Court has developed a large body of law ("Constitutional Law") while interpreting that relatively short document known as the Constitution of the United States. State courts are engaged in the same process.

Reporters

I. Opinion → Report → Reporter

The rules of law being made by a court are found in its published opinions.

An opinion is an appellate court's written explanation of why it affirmed, reversed, or modified the holding of the trial court. It gives some indication of the facts of the case, the applicable rules of law, the issues[4] and how and why the rules apply to the facts (the "holding"). An opinion is the main element in a report.[5] The other elements are indicated below.

A report is found in a set of books called a reporter. A reporter contains reports of cases from a single court or related courts, in chronological order as they are decided.

If you now realize that the courts have an important lawmaking function, that precedents go back to fifteenth century England, and that there are fifty-one jurisdictions in the United States, you now know why law libraries have thousands of volumes of reporters. It remains to go into some detail of the structure of these reports and the various series of reporters in which they are found.

II. The Elements of a Case Report

Go to the law library, take down a reporter volume, and note the following elements in the report of almost any case. (If you do not have easy access to a law library, refer to illustrations 1a–1e. But, you are far more likely to fix these elements in your mind if you see them in the flesh, in the reporters.)

---

4. "Issues" are the questions raised where the rules of law impinge on the facts of the case.
5. Reports are also called "cases," "opinions," and "decisions."

(1) TITLE. (*E.g. Hoskins* v. *Morgan.*) This is also called "Name of the Case."

(2) DOCKET NUMBER. (*E.g.* Civ. 80–1373 or Crim. 85–914.) Courts simply assign numbers consecutively to their cases. Frequently, there are two numbers at the beginning indicating the year.

(3) NAME OF THE COURT.

(4) DATE OF THE DECISION.

(5) SUMMARY OF THE CASE. This is also called a "syllabus." It recounts what happened "below" (lower court) and states the central holding of this court.

(6) HEADNOTES. These are also called "digests" or, less often, "squibs." They are written by commercial editors or court reporters who more or less mechanically extract excerpts from the opinion that appear to be statements of points of law. Headnotes encompass both holding and dictum. Their primary function is to serve as the basis for a case finding tool called a digest (see p. 35) and also as the case annotations in annotated codes (see p. 59). Occasionally, it is helpful to glance over the headnotes to get some idea of what the case is about before reading the opinion.

(7) NAMES OF THE ATTORNEYS.

(8) THE OPINION. It always starts with the name of the justice[6] who has written it. One of the majority justices is chosen to write the opinion for all (except when one or more decide to write a concurring opinion). This opinion is the official document. Here is where court made law is found. The major portion of a law student's three years in law school is spent in analyzing these opinions in order to determine the principles of law for which they are precedents.

(9) THE ORDER OF THE COURT. (*E.g.* "Judgement is affirmed.")

(10) THE NAMES OF THE CONCURRING JUSTICES. Sometimes there is also a concurring opinion/s.

(11) THE DISSENTING OPINION/S. Of course, if the justices vote unanimously, there will be no dissenting opinion. Dissenting opinions may not be cited as binding authority; however, they may be cited as persuasive authority, especially if the court is fairly evenly divided.

(12) THE NAMES OF THE DISSENTING JUSTICES (if any).

---

6. An appellate court judge generally has the title of "justice."

Illustrations 1a-1e. A Report of a Case.

SUPREME COURT REPORTER

VOLUME 74

COVERING

VOLUMES 346–347 U. S. REPORTS

CASES ARGUED AND DETERMINED

IN THE

SUPREME COURT OF THE UNITED STATES

OCTOBER TERM, 1953

ST. PAUL, MINN.

WEST PUBLISHING CO.

1954

Illustration 1a. Title page from West's *Supreme Court Reporter,* Volume 74. Copyright © 1954 by West Publishing Company. Reprinted with permission.

686   74 SUPREME COURT REPORTER   [347 U.S.]

Parallel citation ———— 347 U.S. 483
BROWN et al.
v.
BOARD OF EDUCATION OF TOPEKA,
SHAWNEE COUNTY, KAN., et al.

Title or
name of   BRIGGS et al.   v.   ELLIOTT et al.
case   DAVIS et al.
v.
COUNTY SCHOOL BOARD OF PRINCE
EDWARD COUNTY, VA., et al.

GEBHART et al.   v.   BELTON et al.

Docket no. ————————→ Nos. 1, 2, 4, 10.

Reargued Dec. 7, 8, 9, 1953.

Date ————————————→ Decided May 17, 1954.

Class actions originating in the four
states of Kansas, South Carolina, Virginia, and Delaware, by which minor
Negro plaintiffs sought to obtain admission to public schools on a nonsegregated basis. On direct appeals by plaintiffs from adverse decisions in the United States District Courts, District of
Kansas, 98 F.Supp. 797, Eastern District
of South Carolina, 103 F.Supp. 920, and
Eastern District of Virginia, 103 F.Supp.
337, and on grant of certiorari after de-
Syllabus   cision favorable to plaintiffs in the Su-
or   preme Court of Delaware, 91 A.2d 137,
summary   the United States Supreme Court, Mr.
of the   Chief Justice Warren, held that segrega-
case   tion of children in public schools solely
on the basis of race, even though the
physical facilities and other tangible
factors may be equal, deprives the children of the minority group of equal
educational opportunities, in contraven-
tion of the Equal Protection Clause of
the Fourteenth Amendment.

Cases ordered restored to docket for
further argument regarding formulation of decrees.

1. Constitutional Law ⇐47
In resolving question whether segregation of races in public schools consti-
Headnote   tuted a denial of equal protection of the
laws, even though the tangible facilities
provided might be equal, court would

consider public education in light of its
full development and present status
throughout the nation, and not in light
of conditions prevailing at time of adoption of the amendment. U.S.C.A.Const.
Amend. 14.

2. Constitutional Law ⇐220
The opportunity of an education,
where the state has undertaken to provide it, is a right which must be made
available to all on equal terms. U.S.C.A.
Const. Amend. 14.

3. Constitutional Law ⇐220
The segregation of children in public schools solely on the basis of race,
even though the physical facilities and
other tangible factors may be equal, deprives the children of minority group of
equal educational opportunities, and
amounts to a deprivation of the equal
protection of the laws guaranteed by the
Fourteenth Amendment to the Federal
Constitution. U.S.C.A.Const. Amend. 14.

4. Constitutional Law ⇐220
The doctrine of "separate but equal"
has no place in the field of public education, since separate educational facilities
are inherently unequal. U.S.C.A.Const.
Amend. 14.

5. Appeal and Error ⇐819
In view of fact that actions raising
question of constitutional validity of
segregation of races in public schools
were class actions, and because of the
wide applicability of decision holding
that segregation was denial of equal
protection of laws, and the great variety
of local conditions, the formation of decrees presented problems of considerable
complexity, requiring that cases be restored to the docket so that court might
have full assistance of parties in formulating appropriate decrees. U.S.C.A.
Const. Amend. 14.

No. 1:
484
Mr. Robert L. Carter, New York City,
for appellants Brown and others.

Illustration 1b. First page of *Brown v. Board of Education of Topeka*.
From West's *Supreme Court Reporter*, Volume 74. S. Ct. 686. Copyright ©
1954 by West Publishing Company. Reprinted with permission.

Citation title

Attorneys

Mr. Paul E. Wilson, Topeka, Kan., for appellees Board of Education of Topeka and others.

Nos. 2, 4:

Messrs. Spottswood Robinson III, Thurgood Marshall, New York City, for appellants Briggs and Davis and others.

Messrs. John W. Davis, T. Justin Moore, J. Lindsay Almond, Jr., Richmond, Va., for appellees Elliott and County School Board of Prince Edward County and others.

Asst. Atty. Gen. J. Lee Rankin for United States amicus curiae by special leave of Court.

No. 10:

485

Mr. H. Albert Young, Wilmington, Del., for petitioners Gebhart et al.

Mr. Jack Greenberg, Thurgood Marshall, New York City, for respondents Belton et al.

486

Mr. Chief Justice WARREN delivered the opinion of the Court.

Opinion starts here

These cases come to us from the States of Kansas, South Carolina, Virginia, and Delaware. They are premised on different facts and different local conditions, but a common legal question justifies their consideration together in this consolidated opinion.[1]

1. In the Kansas case, Brown v. Board of Education, the plaintiffs are Negro children of elementary school age residing in Topeka. They brought this action in the United States District Court for the District of Kansas to enjoin enforcement of a Kansas statute which permits, but does not require, cities of more than 15,000 population to maintain separate school facilities for Negro and white students. Kan.Gen.Stat.1949, § 72–1724. Pursuant to that authority, the Topeka Board of Education elected to establish segregated elementary schools. Other public schools in the community, however, are operated on a nonsegregated basis. The three-judge District Court, convened under 28 U.S.C. §§ 2281 and 2284, 28 U.S.C.A. §§ 2281, 2284, found that segregation in public education has a detrimental effect upon Negro children, but denied relief on the ground that the Negro and white schools were substantially equal with respect to buildings, transportation, curricula, and educational qualifications of teachers. 98 F.Supp. 797. The case is here on direct appeal under 28 U.S.C. § 1253, 28 U.S.C.A. § 1253.

In the South Carolina case, Briggs v. Elliott, the plaintiffs are Negro children of both elementary and high school age residing in Clarendon County. They brought this action in the United States District Court for the Eastern District of South Carolina to enjoin enforcement of provisions in the state constitution and statutory code which require the segregation of Negroes and whites in public schools. S.C.Const. Art. XI, § 7; S.C. Code 1942, § 5377. The three-judge District Court, convened under 28 U.S.C. §§

2281 and 2284, 28 U.S.C.A. §§ 2281, 2284, denied the requested relief. The court found that the Negro schools were inferior to the white schools and ordered the defendants to begin immediately to equalize the facilities. But the court sustained the validity of the contested provisions and denied the plaintiffs' admission to the white schools during the equalization program. 98 F.Supp. 529. This Court vacated the District Court's judgment and remanded the case for the purpose of obtaining the court's views on a report filed by the defendants concerning the progress made in the equalization program. 342 U.S. 350, 72 S.Ct. 327, 96 L.Ed. 392. On remand, the District Court found that substantial equality had been achieved except for buildings and that the defendants were proceeding to rectify this inequality as well. 103 F. Supp. 920. The case is again here on direct appeal under 28 U.S.C. § 1253, 28 U.S.C.A. § 1253.

In the Virginia case, Davis v. County School Board, the plaintiffs are Negro children of high school age residing in Prince Edward County. They brought this action in the United States District Court for the Eastern District of Virginia to enjoin enforcement of provisions in the state constitution and statutory code which require the segregation of Negroes and whites in public schools. Va.Const. § 140; Va.Code 1950, § 22–221. The three-judge District Court, convened under 28 U.S.C. §§ 2281 and 2284, 28 U.S.C.A. §§ 2281, 2284, denied the requested relief. The court found the Negro school inferior in physical plant, curricula, and transportation, and ordered the defendants

Illustration 1c. From the report of the *Brown* case. From West's *Supreme Court Reporter*, Volume 74. Copyright © 1954 by West Publishing Company. Reprinted with permission.

692   74 SUPREME COURT REPORTER   [347 U.S.]

Whatever may have been the extent of psychological knowledge at the time of Plessy v. Ferguson, this finding is amply supported by modern authority.[11] Any language

495

in Plessy v. Ferguson contrary to this finding is rejected.

[4] We conclude that in the field of public education the doctrine of "separate but equal" has no place. Separate educational facilities are inherently unequal. Therefore, we hold that the plaintiffs and others similarly situated for whom the actions have been brought are, by reason of the segregation complained of, deprived of the equal protection of the laws guaranteed by the Fourteenth Amendment. This disposition makes unnecessary any discussion whether such segregation also violates the Due Process Clause of the Fourteenth Amendment.[12]

[5] Because these are class actions, because of the wide applicability of this decision, and because of the great variety of local conditions, the formulation of de-

crees in these cases presents problems of considerable complexity. On reargument, the consideration of appropriate relief was necessarily subordinated to the primary question—the constitutionality of segregation in public education. We have now announced that such segregation is a denial of the equal protection of the laws. In order that we may have the full assistance of the parties in formulating decrees, the cases will be restored to the docket, and the parties are requested to present further argument on Questions 4 and 5 previously propounded by the Court for the reargument this Term.[13] The Attorney General

496

of the United States is again invited to participate. The Attorneys General of the states requiring or permitting segregation in public education will also be permitted to appear as *amici curiae* upon request to do so by September 15, 1954, and submission of briefs by October 1, 1954.[14]

It is so ordered.

---

are substantially inferior to those available to white children otherwise similarly situated." 87 A.2d 862, 865.

11. K. B. Clark, Effect of Prejudice and Discrimination on Personality Development (Midcentury White House Conference on Children and Youth, 1950); Witmer and Kotinsky, Personality in the Making (1952), c. VI; Deutscher and Chein, The Psychological Effects of Enforced Segregation: A Survey of Social Science Opinion, 26 J.Psychol. 259 (1948); Chein, What are the Psychological Effects of Segregation Under Conditions of Equal Facilities?, 3 Int. J. Opinion and Attitude Res. 229 (1949); Brameld, Educational Costs, in Discrimination and National Welfare (MacIver, ed., 1949), 44–48; Frazier, The Negro in the United States (1949), 674–681. And see generally Myrdal, An American Dilemma (1944).

12. See Bolling v. Sharpe, 347 U.S. 497, 74 S.Ct. 693, concerning the Due Process Clause of the Fifth Amendment.

13. "4. Assuming it is decided that segregation in public schools violates the Fourteenth Amendment

"(a) would a decree necessarily follow providing that, within the limits set by

normal geographic school districting, Negro children should forthwith be admitted to schools of their choice, or

"(b) may this Court, in the exercise of its equity powers, permit an effective gradual adjustment to be brought about from existing segregated systems to a system not based on color distinctions?

"5. On the assumption on which questions 4(a) and (b) are based, and assuming further that this Court will exercise its equity powers to the end described in question 4(b),

"(a) should this Court formulate detailed decrees in these cases;

"(b) if so, what specific issues should the decrees reach;

"(c) should this Court appoint a special master to hear evidence with a view to recommending specific terms for such decrees;

"(d) should this Court remand to the courts of first instance with directions to frame decrees in these cases, and if so what general directions should the decrees of this Court include and what procedures should the courts of first instance follow in arriving at the specific terms of more detailed decrees?"

14. See Rule 42, Revised Rules of this Court, effective July 1, 1954, 28 U.S.C.A.

Headnotes 4 and 5 came from here *case*

Page in Official Reporter ("Star Paging")

Illustration 1d. From the report of the *Brown* case. From West's *Supreme Court Reporter*, Volume 74. Copyright © 1954 by West Publishing Company. Reprinted with permission.

[347 U.S.] BOLLING v. SHARPE 693
Cite as 74 S.Ct. 693

The court's order — Cases ordered restored to docket for further argument on question of appropriate decrees.

2. Constitutional Law ⬅209, 251

The concepts of equal protection of the laws and due process both stem from the American ideal of fairness, and are not mutually exclusive, nor are the concepts always interchangeable, in that equal protection of the laws is a more explicit safeguard of prohibited unfairness than due process of law, but a discrimination may nevertheless be so unjustifiable as to be violative of due process. U.S.C.A.Const. Amends. 5, 14.

3. Constitutional Law ⬅215

Classifications based solely upon race are to be scrutinized with particular care, in that they are contrary to American traditions and constitutionally suspect. U.S.C.A.Const. Amends. 5, 14.

347 U.S. 497
BOLLING et al. v. SHARPE et al.
No. 8.

Reargued Dec. 8, 9, 1953.

Decided May 17, 1954.

Class action by which minor Negro plaintiffs sought to obtain admission to public schools on a nonsegregated basis. The United States District Court for the District of Columbia dismissed complaint, and plaintiffs were granted certiorari by the Supreme Court before judgment on appeal to the United States Court of Appeals for the District of Columbia. The Supreme Court, Mr. Chief Justice Warren, held that the segregation in public education of children because of race is not reasonably related to any proper governmental objective, and thus such segregation in the District of Columbia imposed upon segregated Negro children, even if they were provided with equal physical facilities, a burden constituting an arbitrary deprivation of their liberty in violation of the Due Process Clause of the Fifth Amendment to the Federal Constitution.

Case ordered restored to docket for reargument on questions relative to formulation of appropriate decree in accordance with opinion.

1. District of Columbia ⬅2

The Fourteenth Amendment to the Federal Constitution, containing the Equal Protection Clause, does not apply to the District of Columbia, but the Fifth Amendment, not containing such clause, is applicable therein. U.S.C.A. Const. Amends. 5, 14.

4. Constitutional Law ⬅215

The Constitution of the United States forbids, so far as civil and political rights are concerned, discrimination by the general government, or by the states, against any citizen because of his race. U.S.C.A.Const. Amends. 5, 14.

5. Constitutional Law ⬅255

The term "liberty" within the Fifth Amendment to the Federal Constitution is not confined to mere freedom from bodily restraint, but it extends to the full range of conduct which the individual is free to pursue, and it cannot be restricted except for a proper governmental objective. U.S.C.A.Const. Amends. 5, 14.

See publication Words and Phrases, for other judicial constructions and definitions of "Liberty".

6. Constitutional Law ⬅255

The segregation in public education of children because of race is not reasonably related to any proper governmental objective, and thus such segregation in the District of Columbia imposed upon the segregated Negro children, even if they were provided with equal physical facilities, a burden constituting an arbitrary deprivation of their liberty in violation of the Due Process Clause of the Fifth Amendment to the Federal

Illustration 1e. Final page of the report of the *Brown* case. From West's *Supreme Court Reporter,* Volume 74. Copyright © 1954 by West Publishing Company. Reprinted with permission.

Illustration 2
The Pattern of Law Reporting in the United States

State		Federal	
Official	Unofficial	Official	Unofficial
		U.S. Supreme Court	
	West's "Regional Reporters" have the following units:	United States Reports	Supreme Court Reporter (West) United States Supreme Court Reports, Lawyers Edition (Lawyers Co-op)
Most states publish their own reporter (e.g., Illinois Reports, Illinois Appellate Court Reports, Oklahoma Reports, etc.)	Atlantic Reporter: Conn., Del., D.C., Maine, Md., N.H., N.J., Pa., R.I., and Vt.		
Some states have adopted the West reporter as the official reporter.	Northeastern Reporter: Ill., Ind., Mass., N.Y.,* and Ohio.		
		U.S. Circuit Courts of Appeals	
	Northwestern Reporter: Iowa, Mich., Minn., Nebr., N. Dak., S. Dak., and Wis.	None	Federal Reporter (West)**
	Pacific Reporter: Alaska, Ariz., Calif.,* Colo., Hawaii, Idaho, Kans., Mont., Nev., N. Mex., Okla., Oreg., Utah, Wash., and Wyo.		
		U.S. District Courts	
	Southeastern Reporter: Ga., N.C., S.C., Va., and W. Va.	None	Federal Supplement (West)**

Southern Reporter:
Ala., Fla., La., and Miss.

Southwestern Reporter:
Ark., Ky., Mo., Tenn., and Tex.

New York Supplement:
Covers all New York appellate
levels.

California Reporter:
Covers all California appellate
levels.

(The Regional Reporters start in
the 1880's)

*Highest court only.

**(Also covers miscellaneous
other federal courts)

III.   **The Pattern of Law Reporting in the United States (Illustration 2).**

At first you may feel overwhelmed by the many reporters in a law library. If you become aware of certain underlying factors, however, you will soon see an overall pattern that will make it easier to remember the coverage of the individual reporters.

One of these underlying factors, of course, is our federal system which gives us reporters for state courts and for federal courts.

Another factor is the distinction between official and unofficial reporters. Most, but not all, states publish their own reporter. Sometimes a state will adopt the West Publishing Company reporter as official. The federal government only publishes the opinions of the United States Supreme Court. These official state and federal reporters must be cited and they do contain the official text.

The unofficial versions are more widely used, however, largely because of their faster publication. The text of the opinion is word-for-word the same in both versions. As you can see from the chart, West covers all states with its Regional Reporters and all federal courts with *Supreme Court Reporter, Federal Reporter,* and *Federal Supplement.* Lawyers Co-op's *"Lawyers Edition"* is an annotated reporter and is discussed on page 24.

The "Regionals" started back in the 1880's. Instead of publishing state by state (i.e. and "Alabama Reporter," "Arizona Reporter," etc.), West grouped the states into seven geographical regions. Later they added New York and California as "regions" of their own. For decisions prior to the start of the Regionals, you only have the official reporters.

IV.   **Reporters for the U.S. Supreme Court: They Illustrate Parallel Reporters, Nominative Reporters, Slip Opinions, Advance Sheets, Star Paging, and Annotated Reporters.**

There are three "parallel reporters" for the United States Supreme Court. Parallel reporters are reporters that overlap in their coverage.[7] By looking at these Supreme Court reporters in some detail, we can illustrate most of the features you might find in the other reporters.

A. *United States Reports* (U.S.)

This is the official reporter for the Supreme Court. If you look at its title page, you can see that it is published by the United States Government Printing Office.

---

7. For example, the decisions of the California Supreme Court are reported in one official reporter (*California Reports*) and two Regional reporters (*California Reporter* and *Pacific Reporter*) Similarly, the decisions of the New York Court of Appeals can be found in the official *New York Reports* and West's *New York Supplement* and *Northeastern Reporter.*

As you look at the spines of the earlier volumes on the shelves, you can see names like "Dallas," "Cranch," "Wheaton," "Peters," *et al.* These are examples of "nominative reporters." Up through the latter part of the nineteenth century, most of the English and American reporters were cited by the name of the reporter rather than the jurisdiction covered (e.g. 4 Dallas 266). All of the nominative Supreme Court reporters have been renumbered into one consecutive "U.S." series.

The *United States Reports* are first published in a form called "slip opinions," which are separate pamphlet bindings of individual cases. They come out a week or two after the decision.

The "advance sheets" for *United States Reports* are called "Preliminary Prints." These paperbound booklets are typical of all advance sheets. They contain recent cases before they are bound in the hard bound volumes. Since the printers use the same plates to print the advance sheets as they do the bound volumes, you can cite cases by their ultimate page and volume numbers as soon as they appear in the advance sheets. This is true of all advance sheets.

B. *Supreme Court Reporter* (S. Ct.)

This is a West Publishing Company reporter. If you look inside one of the older volumes you can see numbers inserted in the text of the opinion, often between sentences. (See Illustration 1d.) In the more recent volumes they put the number in the margin and use an upside down "T" symbol in the text. These numbers tell you precisely where a new page starts in the official reporter. This allows you to accurately cite the official reporter, even though you only have the West reporter. This system is called "star paging," after the early practice of inserting an asterisk or star at the point where a new page began.

At the end of the bound volumes on the shelves you find the *Supreme Court Reporter* advance sheets. As noted earlier, the volume and page numbers continue right on from the bound volumes. They contain a number of tables which also continue on from the bound volumes. The cumulative table of cases is the table you most often use.[8] Check it when you are looking for a recent Supreme Court case and you have the name but not the rest of the citation.

---

8. All of these tables tie in with other West publications. The "table of cases" starts in their digest, continues in the digest supplements, and continues even further in the advance sheets of their reporter. The "table of statutes construed" gives you citations to cases that have construed statutes. It is a way of updating your search for case annotations after you have gone through U.S.C.A. and its supplements (*i.e.* the advance sheets could be even more recent than the U.S.C.A. annotation supplement). The tables of "court rules construed" updates federal court rules services that West publishes. The "table of words and phrases" updates their *Words and Phrases.* The

C. *United States Supreme Court Reports, Lawyers Edition* (L. Ed.)

Another major law book publishing company is the Lawyers Cooperative/Bancroft-Whitney Publishing Co. They publish an important research tool called *American Law Reports* (A.L.R.), which is covered in Chapter 13. Both A.L.R. and *"Lawyers' Edition"* provide "annotations" with the text of the opinions. An annotation, in this sense, is a legal essay on the primary issue raised by the reported case. The writer of the annotation gathers all the cases on the issue from all jurisdictions, analyzes their holdings, and then generalizes the rules of law the courts apply to a particular factual situation.

If you look in the back of one of the more recent volumes of *Lawyers' Edition,* you will see what an annotation is. Note that they also provide star paging with their reports of the opinions.

D. Fast Supreme Court Services

There are two looseleaf services that specialize in fast reporting of the opinions and other activities of the United States Supreme Court.

1. *U.S. Law Week* (U.S.L.W.)

In the "Supreme Court Sections" volume of *U.S. Law Week* you find the full text of the latest decisions of the Supreme Court. The weekly issue is received by a library on a Wednesday or Thursday and contains the text of Supreme Court decisions handed down on Monday (the usual "decision day" for the court). The current docket, journal, orders, and summary of oral arguments round out the full coverage *Law Week* gives to the Supreme Court.[9]

2. *Supreme Court Bulletin*

This Commerce Clearing House service provides approximately the same information on the Supreme Court as *Law Week.* It covers the Supreme Court exclusively.

"Key Number Digest" collects the headnotes that have appeared in the cases reported in the advance sheets. These will be incorporated in West's *United States Supreme Court Digest.*

Note that all these tables are cumulative. *Be alert to cumulations whenever you use supplements.* For example, do not waste your time checking each table of cases in all the advance sheets for one volume number—the latest advance sheet for that volume cumulates the prior tables.

9. *U.S. Law Week* might be called a national legal newspaper. It comes out in two volumes: "Supreme Court Sections" and "General Law Sections." Outside of the Supreme Court, coverage is selective. But it is a good place to check for important federal statutes, federal or state cases, or federal administrative rulings that have not been reported yet elsewhere. The electronic data bases *LEXIS* and *WESTLAW* are even more prompt (see chapter 19).

V. Not all Cases are Reported.

Often people look for cases they have heard about in the news media and are surprised to find that it is not available in a law library. Not all cases are reported.

The biggest category of unreported cases are trial cases. Generally, only cases that have been decided on appeal are reported.[10] Do not forget that the purpose for publishing opinions is to record precedents. Only appellate courts make precedents. A trial judge only decides for the litigating parties. He or she is bound by the precedents set by appellate courts above in the jurisdictional hierarchy, but not by decisions of fellow trial judges.

Not even all appellate cases are reported. Some state court systems[11] and the federal circuit courts only publish opinions that establish new precedents or are of other particular interest.[12]

Correct Citation Form for Reports of Cases

Mathews v. *Weber,* 423 U.S. 261 (1976)

The above citation tells you that the *Mathews* v. *Weber* case was decided in 1976 and can be found in volume 423, starting on p. 261 of the *United States Reports.* The rule is that you do not give the parallel citations for U.S. Supreme Court Cases.

Sevin v. *State Bar,* 8 Cal. 3d 641, 504 P.2d 449, 105 Cal. Rptr. 513 (1973)

The above citation illustrates parallel citation. The same case can be found in the official *California Reports* third series and in the two West reporters: *Pacific Reporter* second series and *California Reporter.*

Zack v. *Smith,* 429 N.E.2d 983 (Ind. Ct. App. 1982)
Godinez v. *Lane,* 733 F.2d 1250 (7th Cir. 1984)
McLean v. *Heckler,* 586 F. Supp. 1364 (E.D. Pa. 1984)

In the above citations, the name of the court is indicated in parentheses because these reporters cover several courts. Every case citation must reveal which court decided the case.

---

10. There are some notable exceptions: federal district court opinions are reported in the *Federal Supplement* and Pennsylvania county court opinions are reported in their "side reports." These opinions are cited as persuasive but not binding authority.

11. Including California, New Jersey, New York, Ohio, Texas, Washington, and others. In general, this restriction on publication only applies to the lower appellate levels.

12. For information on unreported cases, contact the clerk of the court in question. Photocopies are generally available at cost.

Shepard's Citations
(Cases Editions)

I. The Purpose of *Shepard's*

After you have found a case on point, two further questions must be answered before it can be cited as a precedent:

(1) What was the "history of the case"? In other words, what was the subsequent procedural history, if any? If you have a case from the Michigan Court of Appeals, was it appealed to the Supreme Court of Michigan or to the Supreme Court of the United States? Did they reverse, affirm, or modify? Answers to these questions would dramatically effect the value of your case as precedent.

(2) What was the "treatment of the case"? In other words, how did later cases treat your case as precedent? Did they follow it, overrule it, criticize it, or explain it?

Look at the first few introductory pages of any volume of *Shepard's* covering cases and you will find some tables labeled "Abbreviations-Analysis." (Or see Illustration 3b.) The first two tables of abbreviations, dealing with the history and the treatment of a case, reveal the kinds of information *Shepard's* can give about a case.

II. The Steps in "Shepardizing" a Case (Illustrations 3a–3d.)

Step 1. Find the right *Shepard's* series.

There is a *Shepard's* for every reporter. They are either shelved at the end of each of the reporter series they cover or all together in one location in the library. Make sure you have the "case edition" and not the "statute edition."

Step 2. Find the main volume and all of its supplements.

The general pattern is a red, hard bound main volume or volumes; a red, paper bound cumulative supplement; plus a final, uncolored pamphlet advance sheet. Sometimes a gold, paper bound annual supplement will follow the main volume or volumes.

Step 3. Find the volume number of the case citation.

On the top of every page in *Shepard's* you will find the name of the reporter and the volume number.

Step 4. Find the page number of the case citation.

The page numbers of case citations are found in bold face scattered throughout each page of *Shepard's*.

Step 5. Read and study the list of citations under your case.

Shepard's gives a list of all the cases, attorney general opinions, major local and national law reviews, and other sources that have cited your case. Abbreviations at the front of some citations tell whether or not the citing case has affirmed, reversed, modified, followed, or distinguished your case. The small superior numbers in the middle of the citations refer to headnote numbers in your case and, therefore, indicate for which point of law it was cited.

Step 6. Check the tables of abbreviations at the front of *Shepard's*.

No one makes a special effort to memorize the *Shepard's* abbreviations for the history and treatment of cases. There are also tables of abbreviations for the titles of the reporters, law reviews, etc. which you need to refer to because *Shepard's* uses its own truncated abbreviations.

Step 7. Check all the supplements.

Repeat steps 3 through 6 in all of the supplements. Check the "What your library should contain" statement in the latest supplement to be sure you have a complete set.

Illustrations 3a-3d. *Shepard's Citations* **(Cases Editions).**

SHEPARD'S
MICHIGAN CITATIONS

CASES

A COMPILATION OF CITATIONS

TO

MICHIGAN CASES REPORTED IN THE VARIOUS SERIES OF MICHIGAN REPORTS AND IN THE NORTHWESTERN REPORTER

THE CITATIONS

which include affirmances, reversals and dismissals by the Supreme Court of Michigan and the United States Supreme Court

APPEAR IN

HARRINGTON'S CHANCERY REPORTS
WALKER'S CHANCERY REPORTS
DOUGLASS' REPORTS
MICHIGAN REPORTS
MICHIGAN COURT OF APPEALS
  REPORTS
NORTHWESTERN REPORTER
  (Michigan Cases)
BROWN'S NISI PRIUS REPORTS
  (Including Supplements)
HOWELL'S NISI PRIUS CASES
McGRATH'S MANDAMUS CASES
UNITED STATES SUPREME COURT
  REPORTS
LAWYERS' EDITION, UNITED STATES
  SUPREME COURT REPORTS
SUPREME COURT REPORTER
FEDERAL CASES
FEDERAL REPORTER
FEDERAL SUPPLEMENT
FEDERAL RULES DECISIONS
REPORTS OF THE ATTORNEY GENERAL
  OF MICHIGAN
MICHIGAN LAW REVIEW
MICHIGAN STATE BAR JOURNAL
UNIVERSITY OF DETROIT LAW
  JOURNAL

JOURNAL OF URBAN LAW
WAYNE LAW REVIEW
CALIFORNIA LAW REVIEW
COLUMBIA LAW REVIEW
CORNELL LAW QUARTERLY
CORNELL LAW REVIEW
GEORGETOWN LAW JOURNAL
HARVARD LAW REVIEW
LAW AND CONTEMPORARY PROBLEMS
MINNESOTA LAW REVIEW
NEW YORK UNIVERSITY LAW REVIEW
NORTHWESTERN UNIVERSITY LAW
  REVIEW
STANFORD LAW REVIEW
TEXAS LAW REVIEW
UNIVERSITY OF CALIFORNIA AT LOS
  ANGELES LAW REVIEW
UNIVERSITY OF CHICAGO LAW
  REVIEW
UNIVERSITY OF ILLINOIS LAW FORUM
UNIVERSITY OF PENNSYLVANIA LAW
  REVIEW
VIRGINIA LAW REVIEW
WISCONSIN LAW REVIEW
YALE LAW JOURNAL
AMERICAN BAR ASSOCIATION JOURNAL

and in annotations of

LAWYERS' EDITION, UNITED STATES SUPREME COURT REPORTS
AMERICAN LAW REPORTS

also, for Michigan cases reported prior to the Northwestern Reporter or in Howell's Nisi Prius Cases or McGrath's Mandamus Cases, as cited in all units of the National Reporter System and in Vols. 1-283 Illinois Appellate Court Reports, Vols. 1-19 Ohio Appellate Reports and Vols. 1-101 Pennsylvania Superior Court Reports

SEVENTH EDITION - - - - - - - - - - - - - - - - CASES 1978, PART 1

SHEPARD'S, INC.
of
COLORADO SPRINGS
COLORADO 80901

Illustration 3a. Title page from a volume of *Shepard's Michigan Citations-Cases.* From *Shepard's Michigan Citations-Cases,* 7th edition. Copyright © 1978 by McGraw-Hill. Reprinted with permission.

ABBREVIATIONS—ANALYSIS

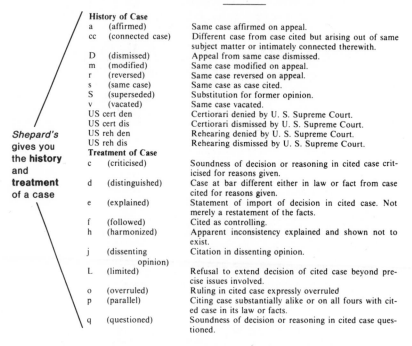

Shepard's gives you the **history** and **treatment** of a case

History of Case

a	(affirmed)	Same case affirmed on appeal.
cc	(connected case)	Different case from case cited but arising out of same subject matter or intimately connected therewith.
D	(dismissed)	Appeal from same case dismissed.
m	(modified)	Same case modified on appeal.
r	(reversed)	Same case reversed on appeal.
s	(same case)	Same case as case cited.
S	(superseded)	Substitution for former opinion.
v	(vacated)	Same case vacated.
US cert den		Certiorari denied by U. S. Supreme Court.
US cert dis		Certiorari dismissed by U. S. Supreme Court.
US reh den		Rehearing denied by U. S. Supreme Court.
US reh dis		Rehearing dismissed by U. S. Supreme Court.

Treatment of Case

c	(criticised)	Soundness of decision or reasoning in cited case criticised for reasons given.
d	(distinguished)	Case at bar different either in law or fact from case cited for reasons given.
e	(explained)	Statement of import of decision in cited case. Not merely a restatement of the facts.
f	(followed)	Cited as controlling.
h	(harmonized)	Apparent inconsistency explained and shown not to exist.
j	(dissenting opinion)	Citation in dissenting opinion.
L	(limited)	Refusal to extend decision of cited case beyond precise issues involved.
o	(overruled)	Ruling in cited case expressly overruled
p	(parallel)	Citing case substantially alike or on all fours with cited case in its law or facts.
q	(questioned)	Soundness of decision or reasoning in cited case questioned.

Illustration 3b. Analysis table from *Shepard's Michigan Citations-Cases*, 7th edition. Copyright © 1978 by McGraw-Hill. Reprinted with permission.

ABBREVIATIONS—REPORTS

A2d–Atlantic Reporter, Second Series
ABA–American Bar Association Journal
AC–Annotated Cases
AD–American Decisions
AG–Reports of the Attorney General
  of Michigan
Æ²–American Law Reports,
  Second Series
Æ³–American Law Reports, Third
  Series
ÆR –American Law Reports
ÆRF –American Law Reports, Federal
AR–American Reports
AS–American State Reports
At–Atlantic Reporter
Brown–Brown's Nisi Prius Reports
BrownS–Brown's Nisi Prius Reports,
  Supplement
CaL–California Law Review
CaR–California Reporter
ChL–University of Chicago Law
  Review
CLA–University of California at Los
  Angeles Law Review
CLQ–Cornell Law Quarterly
Cor–Cornell Law Review
CR–Columbia Law Review
DLJ–University of Detroit Law
  Journal
Doug–Douglass' Reports
F–Federal Reporter
F2d–Federal Reporter, Second Series
FC–Federal Cases
FRD–Federal Rules Decisions
FS–Federal Supplement
Geo–Georgetown Law Journal
HarCh–Harrington's Chancery Reports
HLR–Harvard Law Review
Howell–Howell's Nisi Prius Cases
IlA–Illinois Appellate Court Reports
JUL–Journal of Urban Law, University
  of Detroit Journal of Urban Law
LCP–Law and Contemporary Problems
LCP(3)–Law and Contemporary
  Problems, Part 3
LE–Lawyers' Edition, United States
  Supreme Court Reports
LE²–Lawyers' Edition, United States
  Supreme Court Reports, Second
  Series

IF–University of Illinois Law Forum
Lns–Lawyers Reports Annotated, New
  Series
LRA–Lawyers Reports Annotated
MBJ–Michigan State Bar Journal
McA–Michigan Court of Appeals
  Reports
McGrath–McGrath's Mandamus Cases
Mch–Michigan Reports
McL–Michigan Law Review
MnL–Minnesota Law Review
NE–Northeastern Reporter
NE²–Northeastern Reporter, Second
  Series
NW–Northwestern Reporter
NW²–Northwestern Reporter, Second
  Series
NwL–Northwestern University Law
  Review
NYL–New York University Law
  Review
OA–Ohio Appellate Reports
P–Pacific Reporter
P2d–Pacific Reporter, Second Series
PaL–University of Pennsylvania Law
  Review
PaS–Pennsylvania Superior Court
  Reports
S–New York Supplement
S2d–New York Supplement, Second
  Series
SC–Supreme Court Reporter
SE–Southeastern Reporter
SE²–Southeastern Reporter, Second
  Series
So–Southern Reporter
So2d–Southern Reporter, Second
  Series
StnL–Stanford Law Review
SW–Southwestern Reporter
SW²–Southwestern Reporter, Second
  Series
TxL–Texas Law Review
US–United States Supreme Court
  Reports
VaL–Virginia Law Review
WalkCh–Walker's Chancery Reports
WLR–Wisconsin Law Review
WnL–Wayne Law Review
YLJ–Yale Law Journal

Illustration 3c. Reports table from *Shepard's Michigan Citations-Cases,*
7th edition. Copyright © 1978 by McGraw-Hill. Reprinted with permission.

Volume of Reporter   Name of Reporter

Vol. 186   MICHIGAN REPORTS

Page
in
Reporter

Parallel citation

*another place
to find
text of case refers to.*

headnote.

*explained
earlier ruling*

37McA⁴332	67-68AG80	– 599 –	322Mch¹93	222Mch417	– 49 –	– 83 –	cc199Mch569
j47McA638		(152NW	41-42AG302	222Mch⁷705	(153NW7)	(153NW358)	cc216Mch224
52McA⁸563	– 548 –	1048)		238Mch¹584	242Mch¹50	188Mch¹273	201Mch482
j61McA⁸314	(152NW987)		– 663 –	239Mch¹513	h360Mch¹641	190Mch¹207	219Mch¹73
62McA⁶641	d218Mch¹101	– 614 –	(153NW29)	245Mch⁷402	j360Mch¹643	d197Mch¹264	248Mch¹369
64McA158	j345Mch¹660	(152NW959)	cc139Mch530	253Mch²221	58McA¹682	202Mch¹628	265Mch³375
69McA57		189Mch¹63		253Mch²267		d322Mch¹504	c289Mch461
69McA²718	– 554 –	190Mch¹400	– 672 –	j253Mch³617	– 52 –	396Mch¹271	310Mch370
71McA616	(152NW996)	221Mch¹421	(153NW13)	258Mch⁸358	(153NW4)	37-38AG61	320Mch¹155
273F2d⁴814	371Mch²435	46ЯR1011n	s193Mch200	j261Mch¹171	(LRA¹15E	63-64AG296	326Mch¹360
170FS⁴847			188Mch²210	265Mch³349	314)		
11WnL116	– 564 –	– 617 –	351Mch¹252	273Mch²255	7ЯL1400n	– 88 –	– 165 –
17ЯR159n	(153NW26)	(152NW	26ЯR876n	273Mch²517		(153NW537)	(153NW688)
73ЯR132n		1098)		f275Mch⁷386	– 55 –	cc202Mch536	cc200Mch415
73ЯR145n	– 574 –	277Mch¹10	– 677 –	f275Mch⁸386	(153NW32)	cc202Mch544	
	(152NW	7ЯR1415n	(153NW39)	i280Mch¹135	215Mch¹87	cc207Mch106	– 169 –
– 516 –	1037)				227Mch¹495	194Mch²338	(153NW807)
(152NW	191Mch¹447	– 626 –	186 Mich. 626		250Mch¹331	254Mch¹567	207Mch²504
1096)	195Mch¹677	(153NW14)	was "affirmed"		265Mch¹631	47-48AG705	288Mch533
d196Mch¹345	202Mch¹499	a247US350	on appeal to		266Mch¹223	51-52AG313	289Mch²217
221Mch¹662	217Mch¹510	a62LE1154	U.S. Supreme		276Mch609		
243Mch¹644	217Mch¹514	a38SC495	Court.		17WnL551	– 101 –	– 177 –
253Mch¹374	j307Mch¹386	cc185Mch668				(153NW684)	(153NW799)
285Mch¹628	307Mch¹392	208Mch²217	186 Mich. 634 is		– 62 –		(AC¹18B170)
f320Mch¹127	353Mch¹338	210Mch²10	also reported in		(153NW45)	– 108 –	18McA⁴105
339Mch²218	4ЯR116n	294Mch³288	153 N.W. 10		312Mch¹98	(153NW725)	147ЯR994n
385Mch³9	23ЯR1169n	8WnL130			360Mch¹139	207Mch¹670	78ЯR1314n
j385Mch³23					360Mch140	214Mch³313	78ЯR1353n
q14McA²653	– 577 –	– 634 –			1WnL178	62McA⁴85	9ЯR233n
54McA45	(152NW994)	(153NW10)	360 Mich. 553		1WnL271	54F2d⁴1037	
4ЯR158n		191Mch²386	"explained" the		14ЯR142n	88F2d¹829	– 186 –
	– 583 –	192Mch²196	point of law		i39ЯR1067n	88F2d⁸829	298Mch²545
– 523 –	(152NW979)	197Mch¹348	noted in			508F2d¹304	
(152NW980)		200Mch¹54	headnote #4 in		– 68 –	353FS³107	– 196 –
	– 588 –	206Mch²369	186 Mich. 634		(153NW8)	127ЯR55n	(153NW814)
– 533 –	(152NW993)	206Mch³370			(AC¹18B478)		(LRA¹16F
(152NW972)	(LRA¹16B	209Mch¹19				– 125 –	329)
cc180Mch208	1276)	214Mch⁸70	Vol. 187		– 73 –	(153NW657)	(AC¹16E413)
cc191Mch308	(AC¹17E238)	216Mch⁴554			(153NW5)	(LRA¹16A17)	190Mch⁷11
	f193Mch¹131	c360Mch⁸553	– 1 –		194Mch²119	193Mch¹636	222Mch¹317
– 536 –	194Mch¹105		(153NW1)		204Mch¹325	198Mch¹444	224Mch¹425
(152NW918)	d195Mch¹159	– 640 –	195Mch²156		210Mch¹691	d199Mch²138	233Mch¹386
245Mch²672	199Mch¹86	(153NW12)	225Mch⁸96		215Mch¹188	200Mch⁸296	391Mch¹90
j248Mch²349	201Mch⁴476	284Mch⁸336	1ЯR50n		217Mch⁸566	201Mch¹71	257F¹885
248Mch²355	f212Mch⁸149	336Mch⁸161	84ЯR1359n		242Mch⁸50	201Mch¹195	275F¹904
j262Mch¹21	229Mch¹45	118ЯR1236n			299Mch¹526	201Mch³523	47F2d⁴461
j270Mch²150	252Mch¹645		– 8 –		d314Mch²50	203Mch⁴77	135F2d¹80
275Mch²80	286Mch¹335	– 643 –	(153NW49)		352Mch²537	216Mch⁸350	41FS¹413
j275Mch²192	d333Mch¹710	(153NW11)	188Mch⁸511			216Mch⁸354	82FS¹908
281Mch²649	e383Mch¹729	s192Mch25	191Mch¹367		– 79 –	e217Mch⁸372	56AG474
j283Mch²363	j390Mch¹50	cc192Mch365	191Mch¹369	47ЯR799n	(153NW245)	238Mch¹435	60ЯR998n
286Mch²659	390Mch¹311	194Mch²427	f200Mch⁸205	69ЯR1319n	d197Mch⁸264	250Mch⁸463	
288Mch²394	q390Mch314	197Mch⁸343	204Mch¹437	159ЯR926n	200Mch⁴40	264Mch⁸294	– 206 –
349Mch²339	e6McA¹594	205Mch¹312	209Mch⁷511		202Mch⁸628	264Mch¹297	(153NW913)
	14F2d¹87	235Mch⁸55	212Mch⁸173	– 28 –	233Mch¹361	280Mch⁸295	207Mch⁸524
– 540 –	14WnL366	251Mch¹215	214Mch¹228	(153NW34)	f234Mch⁸430	293Mch⁸213	208Mch187
(152NW950)	21WnL744	15McA¹80	215Mch¹¹463	195Mch¹76	304Mch⁴112	326Mch⁸551	d223Mch²12
cc190Mch195	8ЯR1327n		217Mch⁸317	195Mch¹353	316Mch663	329Mch⁸90	279Mch⁸60
205Mch¹106	24ЯR1468n	– 646 –	218Mch366	195Mch⁸354	j360Mch⁸161	d350Mch⁸108	j38⁷Mch⁸182
236Mch¹342	30ЯR982n	(153NW37)	219Mch¹⁰438	199Mch13	389Mch⁸347	j371Mch⁸628	21McA⁴516
288Mch¹238	67ЯR797n	p186Mch652	220Mch⁸298	215Mch¹689	396Mch⁸270	22F2d⁸941	275F¹582
315Mch¹240	142ЯR829n	33-34AG72		243Mch⁸677	51McA⁴16	87F2d⁴417	24McA⁴744
317Mch¹143		33-34AG93	– 8 –	327Mch²659	35-36AG59	33ЯR1344n	31McA⁴789
63McA¹225	– 593 –	35-36AG375	(153NW49)	56ЯR124n	35-36AG64		64ЯR560n
206FS¹484	(152NW919)	36ЯR950n	188Mch⁸511	72ЯR792n	39-40AG537	– 136 –	84ЯR242n
33-34AG144	s180Mch691		191Mch¹367	77ЯR1168n	41-42AG468	(153NW667)	146ЯR16n
35-36AG313	332Mch¹370	– 652 –	191Mch¹369		43-44AG209	d189Mch²470	50ЯR187n
41-42AG510	333Mch¹647	(153NW39)	f200Mch⁸205	– 38 –	43-44AG322		90ЯR1076n
43-44AG271	364Mch¹40	p186Mch646	204Mch¹437	(153NW3)	47-48AG154	– 140 –	90ЯR1099n
43-44AG281			209Mch⁷511		51-52AG329	(153NW682)	
47-48AG474	– 595 –	– 653 –	212Mch⁸173	– 43 –	56AG417	s194Mch87	– 211 –
51-52AG62	(153NW919)	(153NW23)	214Mch¹228	(153NW359)	57AG248	163ЯR478n	(153NW801)
51-52AG411	cc181Mch274	197Mch362	215Mch¹¹463	s194Mch389	63-64AG122		
52-54AG205	244Mch¹496	204Mch¹453	217Mch⁸317	9ЯR473n	63-64AG296	– 145 –	
65-66AG150	249Mch¹61	204Mch⁴455	218Mch366			(153NW730)	
		304Mch203	219Mch¹⁰438			cc192Mch45	
			220Mch⁸298				

400

III. **Shepard's versus "Blue and White Books" for Finding Parallel Citations**

A. **Shepard's**

Researchers probably turn to *Shepard's* more often for parallel citations because they tend to be more accessible in the library than the "Blue and White Books." If you have the official citation and want the regional citation—go to the *Shepard's* for that official reporter. The regional reporter parallel citation will be in parentheses and will be the first entry in the list of citations. (See Illustration 3d.) Of course, if you have the regional citation and want the official citation—the process is reversed.

B. **"Blue and White Books"**

These are published by West Publishing Co. They are simply tables that take you from official citation to regional citation (blue pages) or vice versa (white pages). Your library can only get white pages for its own state. These tables are faster than *Shepard's* when you have a long list of citations for which you need the parallels.

4

Case Finders

I. **Digests**

A. **What is a Digest? West's *United States Supreme Court Digest for Example.***

A digest is a subject index/abstract to cases. It is not only the way of finding cases by subject, but it is the most comprehensive.[13]

In order to illustrate the workings of a digest, we shall use West's *United States Supreme Court Digest* as an example. It is one of the smaller and more compact digests but it still contains the important features of other digests.

As noted earlier, there is no substitute for your going into a law library and actually looking at the set while it is being explained in the text. If you do not have easy access to these books, see Illustrations 4a–4g.

1. **The Components of a Digest.**

Looking at West's *United States Supreme Court Digest* as it sits on the shelves, you can see that it occupies about two shelves. (Many digests are much larger, the one for all the federal courts occupies about eighteen shelves.)

At the beginning of the set there is a four-volume "Descriptive Word Index." It is simply an index of legal and everyday words that will get you into the main body of the set.

The main body of the set runs from volume 2 to volume 13A and is arranged like an encyclopedia with subjects running from Abandonment to Zoning. Within each of these volumes are page after page of

---

13. Citations to cases on a particular subject can also be found in other research tools, including: annotated codes, practitioners manuals, treatises, law reviews, encyclopedias, annotated reporters, words and phrases, and the electronic data base services. These are all covered later in this work.

short paragraphs that abstract statements of rules of law from U.S. Supreme Court opinions. Each paragraph concludes with a citation to the case from which it came. There are hundreds of thousands of these paragraphs arranged under thousands of sub-topics which are arranged under 422 topics. These paragraphs are called "digests" or "headnotes."

At the end of the set there is a "Table of Cases" volume and a "Defendant-Plaintiff" volume.[14] (The table of cases might also be called a plaintiff-defendant table, which is the usual order of naming the parties.) These tables are used when all you have is the name of a case and want to find its citation. They also can be used as a point of ingress into the digest.

These are the three main components of any digest (*viz.* index volumes, digests volumes, and tables volumes). We will now find out where all those little paragraphs come from.

2. **How a Publisher Constructs a Digest**

It is easier to understand a digest if you know how they are put together. (The following outline of the process is correct in its essentials, but it is not intended as an actual description of how it is done in a particular publishing company.)

The process starts with the reports themselves. Everyday, editors at the publishing company are receiving written opinions from judges all over the United States. Let us pick one opinion and follow it through. We will take the landmark case of *Brown* v. *Board of Education of Topeka* and use the West report of that case to illustrate their digest. So, find the *Brown* case in 74 S. Ct. 686. (Or see Illustrations 1a–1e.) The editor received a copy of this opinion back in 1954. He or she read it through and then proceeded to encircle *every statement in the opinion that appeared to be a statement of a rule of law.* For example, on page 692 (Illustration 1d), the first complete paragraph starts out:

> We conclude that in the field of public education the doctrine of
> "separate but equal" has no place. Separate educational facilities
> are inherently unequal.

The editor interpreted these two sentences as a statement of law and encircled them. They then became a headnote. Look at headnote number four in front of the opinion and you will see the almost identical language of the quote.[15] (See Illustration 1b.) The editors only make such changes

---

14. If your set has volumes 16 and 17 "Rules"—ignore them, they were an added feature to this particular set and not part of the digest itself.

15. You might also note that the headnote includes a citation to the fourteenth amendment. Since constitutions are included along with legislation in annotated codes, this identical headnote will appear as an annotation in West's *United States Code Annotated*.

in the wording as are necessary for smooth, coherent reading as a headnote. The next step is to classify the headnote. In other words, to determine its subject classification. The West Publishing Company has classified American law into over 400 topics which break down into many thousands of subtopics. You can find the topics listed at the beginning of any of the digest volumes. The scheme of subtopics, sub-subtopics, etc. for each topic is set forth in an "Analysis" at the beginning of the topic. A general analysis is followed by a detailed analysis. (See Illustrations 4d and 4e.) Each unique topic, subtopic, etc. combination gets a "Key Number." In our example, headnote number 4 was classified under "Constitutional Law Key Number 220."

Now we have a report of a case that includes headnotes. The next step is to assemble the headnotes from the *Brown* case and all the other U.S. Supreme Court cases within a certain time span, arrange them in classification order, and simply print them in the digest. Open up volume five (copyright 1967) of West's *United States Supreme Court Digest,* and look at "Constitutional Law key number 220." (Or see Illustrations 4c–4g) There you will find all of the cases that have had headnotes classified under that key number. At the bottom of the second column on page 424 you can see, word-for-word, the same paragraph that we saw earlier as headnote number 4 in the *Brown* case. (Illustration 4g.)

B. Caveat: Not Every Headnote is a Holding.

Since determining the holding/s of a case is a complex, time consuming process and one that is subject to varying interpretations, the editors simply make headnotes of every statement that *might* be a holding. Therefore, when you are using a digest, you cannot be sure you have found a "case on point" merely because the language in the headnote appears to be apt. You have to read that case to see if the stated rule was even at issue. Most of these headnotes are dicta. Sometimes the editors will assign twenty to thirty headnotes to a case under a dozen or more key numbers. No case could be precedent for so many rules of law. **Do not cite from headnotes.**

C. The Pattern of Publication of Digests

Since the West Publishing Company, through its "National Reporter System," is preparing headnotes for all reported cases throughout the United States, it has the foundation for an equally comprehensive digesting system. West publishes state digests, regional digests, a federal digest, the *U.S. Supreme Court Digest,*[16] and one grand digest that incorporates them all: *The Decennial Digest.* If you wanted to, you could follow the path of a single headnote that originated in an Ohio case in

16. Lawyers Co-operative Publishing Company also publishes a *U.S. Supreme Court Digest.*

the *North Eastern Reporter* to the *Ohio Digest,* to the *North Eastern Digest,* and ultimately, to the *Decennial Digest.*

D. The *Decennial Digest*

This is also called *The American Digest.* You will probably not use this tool very often because you will seldom be looking for cases from all jurisdictions. State courts want to hear about their own cases.

But, the *Decennial Digest* can be useful on occasion and you should have a general understanding of its unique structure. It has an enormous scope: all reported American cases, state and federal, from 1658 to the present. In order to make this tool manageable, West has divided it into ten year periods. If you will look at the *Decennial Digest* in the library, you will see that it starts with some volumes labeled *Century Edition, 1658 to 1896.* These are followed by the *Decennial Edition, 1897 to 1906,* the *2d Decennial Edition, 1907 to 1916,* and so forth up to the *Eighth Decennial Digest, 1966 to 1976.*

Each of these "Decennials" is a separate and complete digest for a ten year period. Each covers all topics from Abandonment to Zoning. Each is followed by its own table of cases and its own descriptive word index.

The only complication in using this digest is in looking for cases within the current 1976–1986 period. It is the period of the "Ninth Decennial" and the first five years of it are covered by the *Ninth Decennial Digest, Part 1, 1976–1981.* It is a separate and complete digest for its five year period. The 1981–1986 period is being covered by *West's General Digest, Sixth Series.* The *Sixth Series* consists of a series of bound volumes, approximately ten per year, each with its own index and table of cases. Cumulative indexes are being included in each tenth volume.

E. West's Federal Digests

Again, because a digest becomes too cumbersome when it exceeds a certain size, West has broken down its digest of federal cases into four separate series. The first is called the *Federal Digest* and covers the period through 1938. Then, to the lasting confusion of beginning legal researchers, they changed the name to *Modern Federal Practice Digest,* and continued on from 1939 through 1961. (The scope of both is the same, despite the connotations of "practice.") *Federal Practice Digest 2d* covers 1961 to 1975. The current *Federal Practice Digest 3d* covers from 1975 to date. These four series encompass all the federal courts, including the Supreme Court.

F. The Steps in Using a Digest

There are three approaches to using a digest: by index, by analysis of the legal concept, or by case headnotes.

1. **Index Approach**

Most law students and attorneys use the index approach. The steps are:

Step 1. Select the correct digest. (state, regional, federal, etc.)

Step 2. Find the "Descriptive Word Index." (Illustration 4a.)

Step 3. Look under all the terms you think would cover your problem. (Illustration 4b.) Indexes use practical, everyday words (stepladders, truck drivers, etc.) as well as legal terms.[17]

Step 4. Note the "Key numbers" given in the index. (Illustration 4b.)

Step 5. Look over the digests of cases under the key number and find the cases with facts or issues that appear to resemble your problem. (Illustrations 4f and 4g.)

Step 6. Check all supplements. (Pocket part and pamphlet at the end of the set.)

Step 7. Record the case citations and look them up to see if they are *really* on point. Merely using "good quotes" from the digest will get you in trouble. **Do not cite from headnotes.**

2. **Analytic Approach**

You use the analytic approach when you know the general area of the law in question. It is hierarchical—from the general to the specific.

Step 1. Select the correct digest (state, regional, federal, etc.).

Step 2. Select the volume containing your topic, *e.g.* "Constitutional Law." (Illustration 4c.)

Step 3. Read the general or detailed "Analysis" on the first page of the topic. (Illustrations 4d and 4e.)

Step 4. Select the subtopic, *e.g.* "Equal Protection of Laws." (Illustration 4e.)

Step 5. Select the sub-subtopic, *e.g.* "Public Schools." (Illustration 4e.)

Step 6. Look over the digests of cases under the sub-subtopic and find the cases with facts or issues that appear to resemble your problem. (Illustrations 4f and 4g.)

Step 7. Check all supplements. (Pocket part and the pamphlet at the end of the set.)

Step 8. Record the case citations and look them up to see if they are *really* on point. Merely using "good quotes" from the digest will get you in trouble. **Do not cite from headnotes.**

---

17. In trying to find the best index term, do not think of your problem from just one angle. The key term could arise from: the persons involved, the activity engaged in, the instrumentality used, the place in which it occurred, the kind of legal action brought, the defense asserted, or the relief prayed for.

3. Case Headnote Approach

The case headnote approach can be used when you already have one case on point and you want to find others. Simply check the headnotes in the West report of the case and find the key number in which you are interested. Look under that key number in the appropriate West digest.

II. Other Case Finders

In actual practice, lawyers find most of their cases through sources other than a digest. These sources are all covered elsewhere in the text, but should be mentioned here so that you do not limit your thinking to digests when you are looking for cases. No matter where you find your cases, DON'T FORGET TO SHEPARDIZE. Citing an overruled case is embarrassing.

A. Automated Legal Data Bases

Offices that subscribe to *LEXIS* or *WESTLAW* services will do just about all of their case searching at their computer terminals. See Chapter 19.

B. Commentaries

Since all legal writing is heavily annotated, commentaries are good case finders. For example, if you have found a law review article, text book, or looseleaf service on your problem, the writer probably will have already located and analyzed the best cases for you. Commentaries are covered in Section 3.

C. *Words and Phrases*

West Publishing Company made further use of its headnotes and compiled those defining a word or phrase into a set of books called *Words and Phrases*. Do not overlook this unique case finder.

D. Popular Name Tables

When the only citation you have is the "Flag Salute Cases," you need a popular names table. The most complete listing is *Shepard's Acts and Cases by Popular Names, Federal and State*.[18]

E. Annotated Codes

If your problem relates to a section of the statutes, the case notes in the annotated codes will be your best case finder. These are covered in Section 2.

---

18. Popular case name tables can also be found in some of the table of cases volumes of West's *Decennial Digests* and in their *Supreme Court Digest*.

Illustrations 4a–4g. A West Digest.

UNITED STATES

SUPREME COURT DIGEST

1754 TO DATE

Covering
Every Decision of the
Supreme Court of the United States
From Earliest Times to Date

Volume 1C

DESCRIPTIVE – WORD INDEX

R – Z

ST. PAUL, MINN.

WEST PUBLISHING CO.

Illustration 4a. Title page from West's *United States Supreme Court Digest*, Volume 1C. Copyright © 1982 by West Publishing Company. Reprinted with permission.

1C S Ct D—169   **SELF–DEFENSE**

> **References are to Digest Topics and Key Numbers**

SEDUCTION—Cont'd
SENTENCE and punishment. **Seduct 53**
STATUTORY provisions. **Seduct 2, 30**
TRIAL—
  Civil action. **Seduct 23-26**
  Criminal prosecution. **Seduct 47-51**
VERDICT—
  Civil action. **Seduct 26**
  Criminal prosecution. **Seduct 51**

SEEDS
CUSTOM duties. **Cust Dut 30**
LIENS. **Agric 10-15**
PRODUCTS liability. **Prod Liab 45**
WARRANTIES—
  Damages for breach. **Sales 442(11)**

SEEPAGE
DAMS or conduits. **Waters 172**
DRAINAGE or discharge of surface waters. **Waters 119(5)**
STATES, weight and sufficiency of evidence on seepage claims. **States 184.19**

SEGREGATION
CONSTITUTIONALITY of statute, persons entitled to raise questions. **Const Law 42**
LIBRARIES, breach of peace. **Breach of P 1**
NEGROES, generally, see this index **Negroes**
PRIVATE schools, denial of admission to Negro students due to race, permissibility—
  Civil R 3, 8.1
  Const Law 82, 83(2), 91
SCHOOLS and school districts—
  Const Law 220
  Schools 13, 151, 154
Determination of constitutional questions, scope of inquiry. **Const Law 47**
Equal protection of laws. **Const Law 220**

SEINES
BUZZARD'S bay—
  Power to regulate use. **Fish 8**
VALIDITY of act prohibiting use. **Fish 9**

SEISIN
COVENANTS, see this index **Covenants**
CURTESY, seisin of husband or wife as requisite. **Dower & C 4**
DOWER affected by seisin. **Dower & C 5**
INTESTATE'S property, seisin affecting course of descent. **Des & Dist 10-16**
PROPERTY. **Propty 10**

SEIZE AND DESIST ORDERS
MANUFACTURER, truck-load discounts, stay, Federal Trade Commission's refusal to grant. **Trade Reg 925**

SEIZURE
See this index **Searches and Seizures**

SELECTION
ALLOWANCES to surviving spouse or children. **Ex & Ad 191**
COUNSEL by accused. **Crim Law 641.10**
DOWER, property for assignment. **Dower & C 83**
DRAFTS for armed services, generally, see this index **Drafts for Armed Services**
EXECUTION, property to be levied on. **Execution 128**
EXEMPT property—
  Bankr 400(2)
  Exemp 126
  Homestead. Homestead, generally, post
GOODS sold, see this index **Sales**
GRAND jury. **Gr Jury 8**
  Discrimination, burden of proof. **Jury 120**
HOMESTEAD. **Home 29-57½, 150, 196**

SELECTION—Cont'd
JURY—
  Additional jurors or talesman. **Jury 72(6)**
  Compensation of sheriff or constable. **Sheriffs 53**
  Discretion, review of. **Crim Law 1152(2)**
  Discrimination, burden of proof. **Jury 120**
  Errors and irregularities. **Jury 82(2, 3)**
  Excusing or discharging jurors. **Jury 75(4)**
  Full panel to select from. **Jury 80**
  Infringement of right to trial by jury. **Jury 33**
  Necessity of determination of constitutionality of law relating to selection. **Const Law 46**
  Negroes—
    Disparity between tax digest and venires. **Crim Law 322**
  Presentation of questions by record, review dependent on. **Crim Law 1115(2)**
  Presumptions on appeal or writ of error. **Crim Law 1144.8**
  Regular panel. **Jury 66**
  Remarks and conduct of judge. **Crim Law 655(4)**
  Right to particular juror or jury. **Jury 79(3)**
  Scope and extent of review. **Crim Law 1134(5)**
  Titles of laws affecting. **Statut 124(3)**
PUBLIC lands—
  Railroad land grants. **Pub Lands 82**
  Swamp lands. **Pub Lands 59, 60, 61(2)**
RECEIVER, see this index **Receivers**
REFEREE, see this index **References and Referees**
SALES, see this index **Sales**
TELEVISION and radio programs by broadcaster. **Tel 430**
TEXTBOOKS. **Schools 167**
WILLS, see this index **Wills**

SELECTIVE SERVICE
DRAFTS for armed services, generally, see this index **Drafts for Armed Services**
DUE process. **Const Law 255(3)**

SELECTMEN
TOWNS and townships, see this index **Towns**

SELF–DEFENSE
ASSAULT—
  Civil action. **Assault 13, 30**
  Criminal prosecution—
    Assault 67, 96(3)
    Homic 96
CONTINUANCE for evidence to show. **Crim Law 595(6)**
HOMICIDE, defense to prosecution for. **Homic 108-121**
  Admissibility of evidence. **Homic 186-195**
  Instructions. **Homic 300**
  Killing of husband by wife's paramour. **Homic 112(3)**
  Manner of repelling attack as affecting. **Homic 119**
  Nature and imminence of danger. **Homic 115**
  Nature and purpose of attack. **Homic 110**
  Necessity of act. **Homic 96(2), 117**
  Presumptions and burden of proof. **Homic 151(3)**
  Questions for jury. **Homic 276**
  Renewal of contest. **Homic 121**
  Weight and sufficiency of evidence. **Homic 244**
  Withdrawal after aggression. **Homic 113**
INSTRUCTIONS to jury—
  Crim Law 782(16)
  Homic 300
  Burden of proof. **Crim Law 778(12)**
  Construction. **Homic 300(3)**
  Excluding issues, defenses or evidence. **Homic 300(12-15)**
  Invading province of jury. **Crim Law 763(23)**
  Presumptions. **Crim Law 778(12)**
  Requests for instructions already given. **Crim Law 829(5)**

See Illustration 4f for this reference

Illustration 4b. From West's *United States Supreme Court Digest*, Volume 1C. Copyright © 1982 by West Publishing Company. Reprinted with permission.

UNITED STATES
SUPREME COURT DIGEST

1754 TO DATE

Covering
Every Decision of the
Supreme Court of the United States
From Earliest Times to Date

Volume 5

CONSTITUTIONAL LAW ⇐ 1—250

ST. PAUL, MINN.
WEST PUBLISHING CO.

Illustration 4c. Title page from West's *United States Supreme Court Digest*, Volume 5. Copyright © 1982 by West Publishing Company. Reprinted with permission.

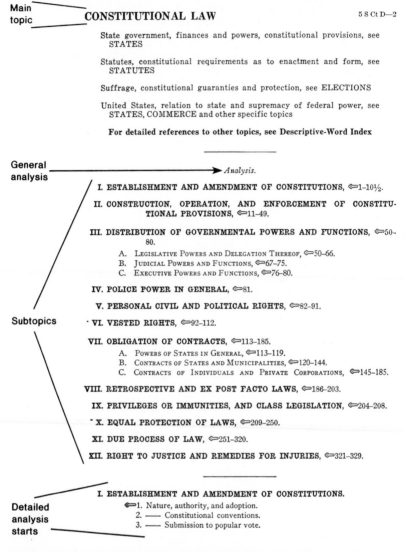

Main topic

CONSTITUTIONAL LAW

5 S Ct D—2

State government, finances and powers, constitutional provisions, see STATES

Statutes, constitutional requirements as to enactment and form, see STATUTES

Suffrage, constitutional guaranties and protection, see ELECTIONS

United States, relation to state and supremacy of federal power, see STATES, COMMERCE and other specific topics

For detailed references to other topics, see Descriptive-Word Index

General analysis

Analysis.

I. ESTABLISHMENT AND AMENDMENT OF CONSTITUTIONS, ☞1–10½.

II. CONSTRUCTION, OPERATION, AND ENFORCEMENT OF CONSTITUTIONAL PROVISIONS, ☞11–49.

III. DISTRIBUTION OF GOVERNMENTAL POWERS AND FUNCTIONS, ☞50–80.
    A. LEGISLATIVE POWERS AND DELEGATION THEREOF, ☞50–66.
    B. JUDICIAL POWERS AND FUNCTIONS, ☞67–75.
    C. EXECUTIVE POWERS AND FUNCTIONS, ☞76–80.

IV. POLICE POWER IN GENERAL, ☞81.

V. PERSONAL CIVIL AND POLITICAL RIGHTS, ☞82–91.

Subtopics

VI. VESTED RIGHTS, ☞92–112.

VII. OBLIGATION OF CONTRACTS, ☞113–185.
    A. POWERS OF STATES IN GENERAL, ☞113–119.
    B. CONTRACTS OF STATES AND MUNICIPALITIES, ☞120–144.
    C. CONTRACTS OF INDIVIDUALS AND PRIVATE CORPORATIONS, ☞145–185.

VIII. RETROSPECTIVE AND EX POST FACTO LAWS, ☞186–203.

IX. PRIVILEGES OR IMMUNITIES, AND CLASS LEGISLATION, ☞204–208.

X. EQUAL PROTECTION OF LAWS, ☞209–250.

XI. DUE PROCESS OF LAW, ☞251–320.

XII. RIGHT TO JUSTICE AND REMEDIES FOR INJURIES, ☞321–329.

I. ESTABLISHMENT AND AMENDMENT OF CONSTITUTIONS.

Detailed analysis starts

    ☞1. Nature, authority, and adoption.
    2. —— Constitutional conventions.
    3. —— Submission to popular vote.

Illustration 4d. General and detailed analyses of "Constitutional Law." From West's *United States Supreme Court Digest,* Volume 5. Copyright © 1982 by West Publishing Company. Reprinted with permission.

Topic ─────────────────────────────────→ **CONSTITUTIONAL LAW**

IX. PRIVILEGES OR IMMUNITIES, AND CLASS LEGISLATION—Continued.

⟜207. Privileges and immunities of citizens of the several states—Continued.
    (4). Taxation and exemptions.
    (5). Preferences to resident creditors.
    (6). Regulating importation of animals.
    (7). Regulating foreign corporations.
- 208. Class legislation.
    (1). In general.
    (2). Discrimination as to particular localities.
- (3). Discrimination against particular classes of persons in general.
    (4). Discrimination against particular classes of corporations and associations.
    (5). Discrimination against particular classes of municipalities.
    (6). Regulation of trades, professions, and business in general.
    (6½). Protection of labels and trade-marks.
    (7). Regulation of relation of master and servant, and protection of employés.
    (8). Sale of patent rights.
    (9). Sales of goods.
    (10). Nuisances.
    (11). Sunday laws.
    (12). Regulation of factors.
    (13). Regulation of insurance.
    (14). Regulation of local improvements.
    (15). Usury laws.
    (16). Remedies.

Subtopic ──────→ **X. EQUAL PROTECTION OF LAWS.**

⟜209. Constitutional guaranties in general.
210. Persons protected.
211. Nature of discriminations prohibited in general.
212. Exercise of police power in general.
213. Control over governmental agencies in general.
214. Discrimination by reason of race, color, or condition.
215. —— In general.
216. —— Inns and restaurants.
217. —— Theaters and places of amusement.
218. —— Public conveyances.
219. —— Places of business or public resort.
Sub-subtopic ──────→ 220. —— Public schools.
221. —— Constitution of juries.
222. —— Competency as witnesses.
223. —— Punishment of crime.
224. Discrimination by reason of sex.
225. Discrimination as to localities.
    (1). In general.
    (2). Annexation of territory to cities.
226. Exercise of power of eminent domain.
227. —— In general.
228. —— Procedure.

Illustration 4e. Continuation of detailed analysis of "Constitutional Law." From West's *United States Supreme Court Digest,* Volume 5. Copyright © 1982 by West Publishing Company. Reprinted with permission.

For later cases see same Topic and Key Number in Pocket Part

which is claimed to produce the discrimination.

McCabe v. Atchison, T. & S. F. R. Co., 35 S.Ct. 69, 235 U.S. 151, 59 L.Ed. 169.

So much of the Oklahoma separate coach law as permits carriers to provide sleeping cars, dining cars, and chair cars for white persons, and to provide no similar accommodations for negroes, denies the latter the equal protection of the laws guaranteed by U. S.C.A.Const. Amend. 14.

McCabe v. Atchison, T. & S. F. R. Co., 35 S.Ct. 69, 235 U.S. 151, 59 L.Ed. 169.

U.S.Ill. 1941. A railroad's action in refusing to permit negro to ride in first-class Pullman car and compelling him, solely because of his race, to ride in second-class car provided for negroes, although he had paid first-class fare and had offered to pay first-class Pullman charge, was "unjust discrimination" within the Interstate Commerce Act, and was a violation of the Fourteenth Amendment. Pope's Dig.Ark., § 1190; Interstate Commerce Act § 3(1), 49 U.S.C.A. § 3(1); U.S.C.A.Const. Amend. 14.

Mitchell v. U. S., 61 S.Ct. 873, 313 U.S. 80, 85 L.Ed. 1201.

⬅⮕**219. —— Places of business or public resort.**

U.S.Ga. 1963. Police officer's command, given with intent to enforce racial discrimination in park, that Negro defendants should leave city owned park violated Equal Protection Clause of the Fourteenth Amendment. U.S.C.A.Const. Amend. 14.

Wright v. State of Ga., 83 S.Ct. 1240, 373 U.S. 284, 10 L.Ed.2d 349, opinion conformed to 131 S.E.2d 851, 219 Ga. 125.

U.S.Ga. 1966. Where city became trustee of land under will providing that land was to be used as park for white people only but park was maintained for many years by city, was an integral part of city's activities and was granted tax exemption, removal of city as trustee and appointment of private trustees to whom title to park was transferred without change in municipal maintenance did not, under Fourteenth Amendment, authorize segregation in park. U.S.C.A.Const. Amends. 5, 14.

Evans v. Newton, 86 S.Ct. 486, 382 U.S. 296, 15 L.Ed.2d 373, on remand 148 S.E. 2d 329, 221 Ga. 870.

State courts that aid private parties to perform public function of maintaining parks on segregated basis implicate state in conduct proscribed by Fourteenth Amendment. U.S. C.A.Const. Amend. 14.

Evans v. Newton, 86 S.Ct. 486, 382 U.S. 296, 15 L.Ed.2d 373, on remand 148 S.E. 2d 329, 221 Ga. 870.

⬅⮕**220. —— Public schools.**

U.S.Ga. 1899. A decision by a state court, denying an injunction against the maintenance by a board of education of a high school for white children, while failing to maintain one for colored children also, for the reason that the funds were not sufficient to maintain it in addition to needed primary schools for colored children, does not constitute a denial to colored persons of the equal protection of the law or equal privileges of citizens of the United States.

Cumming v. Board of Ed. of Richmond County, 20 S.Ct. 197, 175 U.S. 528, 44 L. Ed. 262.

U.S.Miss. 1927. Chinese citizen held not denied equal protection of law by requiring attendance at colored school furnishing equal educational facilities. U.S.C.A.Const. Amend. 14.

Gong Lum v. Rice, 48 S.Ct. 91, 275 U.S. 78, 72 L.Ed. 172.

U.S.Mo. 1939. That white resident was afforded legal education within state of Missouri while negro resident having the same qualifications was refused it there and was required to go outside state to obtain it, constituted denial of "equal protection of laws," notwithstanding there was but a limited demand in Missouri for the legal education of negroes, and notwithstanding state made provision for payment of tuition outside state for negroes desiring legal training. R.S.1929, §§ 9618, 9622 (V.A.M.S. §§ 175.050, 175.060); Mo.St.Ann.Const. art. 11, § 3; U.S.C.A.Const. Amend. 14

State of Mo., ex rel. Gaines v. Canada, 59 S.Ct. 232, 305 U.S. 337, 83 L.Ed. 208, rehearing denied 59 S.Ct. 356, 305 U.S. 676, 83 L.Ed. 437, conformed to 131 S, W.2d 217, 344 Mo. 1238.

Where state of Missouri afforded legal education within state to white residents, alleged fact that provision made for resident negroes for payment of tuition outside state was a temporary one, and was intended to operate merely pending the establishment of a law department for negroes at Lincoln University, did not excuse the discrimination, since the discrimination might continue for an indefinite period by reason of statutory discretion given to curators of Lincoln University as to the establishment of a law department for negroes. R.S.1929, §§ 9618, 9622, (V.A.M.S. 175.050, 175.060); U.S.C.A.Const. Amend. 14.

State of Mo., ex rel. Gaines v. Canada, 59 S.Ct. 232, 305 U.S. 337, 83 L.Ed. 208, rehearing denied 59 S.Ct. 356, 305 U.S. 676, 83 L.Ed. 437, conformed to 131 S. W.2d 217, 344 Mo. 1238.

Case headnotes classified under "key no. 220 Constitutional Law—Public Schools"

Illustration 4f. From West's *United States Supreme Court Digest,* Volume 5. Copyright © 1982 by West Publishing Company. Reprinted with permission.

⟨⟩220 CONSTITUTIONAL LAW 5 S Ct D—424

For later cases see same Topic and Key Number in Pocket Part

State of Missouri affording legal education within state to white residents was bound to furnish resident negro facilities, within state's borders, for legal education, substantially equal to those which the state there afforded for persons of the white race, whether or not other negroes sought the same opportunity, since negro's right was a personal one. U.S.C.A.Const. Amend. 14.

> State of Mo., ex rel. Gaines v. Canada, 59 S.Ct. 232, 305 U.S. 337, 83 L.Ed. 208, rehearing denied 59 S.Ct. 356, 305 U.S. 676, 83 L.Ed. 437, conformed to 131 S. W.2d 217, 344 Mo. 1238.

A state is under obligation to provide negroes with advantages for higher education substantially equal to the advantages afforded to white students. U.S.C.A.Const. Amend. 14.

> State of Mo., ex rel. Gaines v. Canada, 59 S.Ct. 232, 305 U.S. 337, 83 L.Ed. 208, rehearing denied 59 S.Ct. 356, 305 U.S. 676, 83 L.Ed. 437, conformed to 131 S. W.2d 217, 344 Mo. 1238.

U.S.Okl. 1948. The state of Oklahoma, in conformity with equal protection clause of Fourteenth Amendment, was required to provide qualified Negro applicant with legal education afforded by a state institution and to provide it as soon as it did for applicants of any other group and where admission was denied solely because of applicant's color, mandamus would lie to compel admission. U.S.C. A.Const. Amend. 14.

> Sipuel v. Board of Regents of University of Okl., 68 S.Ct. 299, 332 U.S. 631, 92 L. Ed. 247.

U.S.Okl. 1950. Negro student who was admitted to state supported graduate school for purpose of pursuing studies leading to a doctorate in education was entitled to receive same treatment at hands of state as students of other races, and where he was assigned to seat in classroom in a row specified for colored students, was assigned to a table in library, and assigned to a special table in cafeteria, he was deprived of a personal and present right to equal protection of the laws, and the state-imposed restrictions could not be sustained, even though, after removal of restrictions, he might still be set apart by his fellow students. 70 O.S.1941 §§ 455–457; U. S.C.A.Const. Amend. 14.

> McLaurin v. Oklahoma State Regents for Higher Ed., 70 S.Ct. 851, 339 U.S. 637, 94 L.Ed. 1149.

U.S.Tex. 1950. Under equal protection clause of Fourteenth Amendment, qualified Negro applicant had personal and present right to a legal education equivalent to that offered by state to students of other races. U.S.C.A.Const. Amend. 14.

> Sweatt v. Painter, 70 S.Ct. 848, 339 U.S. 629, 94 L.Ed. 1114, rehearing denied 71 S.Ct. 13, 340 U.S. 846, 95 L.Ed. 620.

Where law school of state university, from which Negro applicant was excluded, was one of the nation's ranking law schools, with a faculty of 16 full time and three part-time professors, a student body of 850, and a library containing over 65,000 volumes, whereas proposed law school for Negroes had no independent faculty or library, and law school thereafter opened for Negroes at state university had a faculty of five full-time professors, a student body of 23, and a library of 16,500 volumes, the educational opportunities offered white and Negro law students by the state were not substantially equal and equal protection clause of Fourteenth Amendment required that applicant be admitted to the regular university law school. Acts 1947, c. 29, § 11, Vernon's Ann.Civ.St.Tex. art. 2643b note; Vernons' Ann.Civ.St.Tex. arts. 2643b, 2719, 2900; Vernon's Ann.St.Tex.Const. art. 7, §§ 7, 14; U.S.C.A.Const. Amend. 14.

> Sweatt v. Painter, 70 S.Ct. 848, 339 U.S. 629, 94 L.Ed. 1114, rehearing denied 71 S.Ct. 13, 340 U.S. 846, 95 L.Ed. 620.

U.S.Del., Kan., S.C., Va. 1954. The opportunity of an education, where the state has undertaken to provide it, is a right which must be made available to all on equal terms. U.S.C.A.Const. Amend. 14.

> Brown v. Board of Ed. of Topeka, Shawnee County, Kan., 74 S.Ct. 686, 347 U.S. 483, 98 L.Ed. 873, 38 A.L.R.2d 1180, opinion supplemented 75 S.Ct. 753, 349 U.S. 294, 99 L.Ed. 1083.

The segregation of children in public schools solely on the basis of race, even though the physical facilities and other tangible factors may be equal, deprives the children of minority group of equal educational opportunities, and amounts to a deprivation of the equal protection of the laws guaranteed by the Fourteenth Amendment to the Federal Constitution. U.S.C.A.Const. Amend. 14.

> Brown v. Board of Ed. of Topeka, Shawnee County, Kan., 74 S.Ct. 686, 347 U.S. 483, 98 L.Ed. 873, 38 A.L.R.2d 1180, opinion supplemented 75 S.Ct. 753, 349 U.S. 294, 99 L.Ed. 1083.

The doctrine of "separate but equal" has no place in the field of public education, since separate educational facilities are inherently unequal. U.S.C.A.Const. Amend. 14.

> Brown v. Board of Ed. of Topeka, Shawnee County, Kan., 74 S.Ct. 686, 347 U.S. 483, 98 L.Ed. 873, 38 A.L.R.2d 1180,

Headnote #4 from the *Brown* case.
(See Illustration 1b.)

Illustration 4g. From West's *United States Supreme Court Digest,* Volume 5. Copyright © 1982 by West Publishing Company. Reprinted with permission.

5

Records and Briefs

When an appeal is filed, the appellant must supply a certain number of copies of the record and the appellate brief. The record includes the pleadings filed below, relevant parts of the trial testimony and, perhaps, some documentary evidence. The brief is the written argument directed to the appellate court. The appellee supplies copies of his or her brief. All these copies will go to the members of the appellate bench, opposing counsel, and to certain depository libraries. Many state, county, law school, and bar association law libraries are depositories for their state's records and briefs (sometimes briefs only). The records and briefs of the United States Supreme Court are widely available in microform.

Appellate briefs are a very popular research tool with attorneys in cities where briefs are available. When they find a case on point, they also get the briefs. These briefs are the product of many hours of research on the issues of the case. Pick someone's brain; there are no rewards for doing things the hard way.

Correct Citation Form

Brief for Appellant at 16, *People* v. *Love,* 132 Mich. App. 423, 346 N.W.2d 534 (1983).

SECTION

Codes

Section Outline

Chapter 10: Treaties
   I. The Importance of Treaty Law for the Average Lawyer
  II. Publications Used in Treaty Research
     A. The Text of the United States Treaties
        1. *Statutes at Large* (Stat.)
        2. *United States Treaties and Other International Agreements* (U.S.T.)
     B. Indexes to United States Treaties
        1. Current Index—*Treaties in Force*
        2. Historical Indexes
           a. *United States Treaties and Other International Agreements Cumulative Index 1776–1949.*
           b. *U.S.T. Cumulative Index 1950–1970.*
     C. "Shepardizing" Treaties
     D. Information on Pending Treaties

Preface: What Do We Mean by "Code"?

This section covers the books that contain a broad range of law sources: constitutions, legislation, administrative regulations, court rules, and treaties. Why are these lumped together?

By codes, we are referring to legal rules that are written in *fixed* and *deliberate* language. This kind of rulemaking is different from court-made precedents ("Cases") because:

(1) The courts are primarily concerned with settling one time disputes between particular individuals or corporate entities. In the process, of course, they are also saying that if another case comes up in the future with essentially the same facts and issues—they will *probably* rule the same. But that is quite different from a legislative or an executive agency laying down a rule that will apply to an entire class of people or entities indefinitely.

(2) Courts do not state their precedents in fixed and deliberate language. The rule of law from a case is found by reading the entire opinion: the court's reasoning within the context of the facts of the case and the procedural history. A quotation from an opinion can be no more than a short-hand summary of how the court applied the law to settle a particular dispute—it has little of the word-for-word, crystallized character or effect of a statute, administrative regulation, constitutional provision, treaty clause, etc.

If we now see why these law sources are different from cases, the remaining question is why call them "codes"? The alliteration with "cases" and "commentaries" is admittedly not accidental; however, there are more natural reasons.

First, everything covered in this section (except treaties) is found in sets of books referred to as codes. Constitutions, statutes, and court rules are found in the federal and state statutory codes (*e.g. United States*

Code Annotated, Utah Code Annotated, etc.). Federal and most state regulations are found in administrative codes (*e.g. Code of Federal Regulations, Pennsylvania Code,* etc.).

Secondly, it is in the nature of any continually growing body of laws that are fixed in written form that they must be systematically compiled by subject, indexed, and regularly revised (repeals and additions). To compile, index, and revise is to *codify.*[19]

---

19. Legal scholars have not agreed on a uniform classification scheme for legal authorities nor the books that contain them. The ramifications of the question go far beyond the scope of this manual. See E. Bodenheimer *Jurisprudence,* Chap. XV, (1962).

CHAPTER

6

Constitutions

I. Federal Constitution

The United States Constitution establishes the governmental framework of the world's oldest current republic. Its amendments set forth our fundamental rights. This document has served as the model for many nations seeking to establish a government based on ultimate power in the people.

By the standards of legal writing, it is a short document—a mere seven thousand words. Apartment leases are longer. Its language is very general and much is left unsaid. Its framers did not have a precise or agreed upon notion of a federal government. It has endured for over two hundred years because the careful and deliberate processes of amendment and judicial interpretation have permitted it to be adapted to a succession of national problems. As you can see in reading constitutional law cases, the language of the Constitution is often a mere catch phrase to categorize a series of cases on the subject.

The text of the U.S. Constitution is most conveniently found in the federal annotated codes which are discussed in the next chapter. Beginning researchers typically look for a unique publication of the Constitution and, indeed, there are many separate printings, but the sources in which it is the easiest to find are the federal annotated codes.

II. State Constitutions

The average state constitution is three times as long as the U.S. Constitution. This is because a state constitution is primarily seen as a document that describes and restricts governmental structure and activity *in detail*. Through the process of voter ratification of constitutional amendments, the people have a more direct role in lawmaking than they do with ordinary legislation. Governmental matters of intense public interest often find their way into state constitutions. From the people's point of view, constitutional provisions have the advantage of being difficult to amend, generally requiring a plebiscite. Because of these factors, state constitutions are long, often antiquated, and full of "statutory detail."

As with the federal constitution, state constitutions are most conveniently located in the state annotated codes.

Correct Citation Form: Constitutions

Federal

U.S. Const. amend. XXV, § 3

State

Mich. Const. art. IX, § 6, cl. 3

7

Annotated Codes

I. Check the Statutes First!

There are no flat rules in legal research. But one that comes close is: *check the statutes first.*

When you are faced with a legal research problem, you often are not sure of where to start. You do not know if there is any applicable law and, if there is, you do not know from where it issued. Are there cases on point? Are there statutes, or regulations, or executive orders, or any other "laws" on your subject?

The best strategy is to determine initially if there is an applicable statute. There are at least two reasons for this. First, generally speaking, statutes are more authoritative than cases, administrative regulations, and other sources of law. The legislative branch has the responsibility for making laws. The courts and administrative agencies have no authority to alter the clear meaning of statutory language. Although your research will typically lead you to many sources, your starting point should be the statute. All else is merely interpretation and effectuation of the purposes of the statute. There are few areas of the law today which are not controlled by statute. Even when court decisions determine the central issue of a problem, legislation generally sets the framework within which the problem must be stated.

A second reason for starting with statutes is that they are found in the most efficient and complete of all legal research tools: the annotated codes.

II. **Session Laws and Annotated Codes**

   A. **Session Laws**

   Legislation is published in a chronological form and in a compiled form.

   Every year Congress meets and passes laws. As you might expect, these enactments are collected and published in annual volumes. This series of volumes is called *United States Statutes at Large*. The pattern for the state legislatures is about the same. The generic name for books that contain the enactments of legislatures in *chronological* order (session by session or year by year) is *session laws*.

   If you will look at *Statutes at Large* on the shelves, (or see Illustrations 5a and 5b) you will see from the spine (back of the book) that for each session they are presently divided into "Public Laws," "Private Laws," "Concurrent Resolutions," "Reorganization Plans," and "Proclamations."[20]

   For a while, at least, you will only be interested in the public laws. Each enactment is given a public law number. The numbers are in consecutive order according to the date of signing by the President; otherwise the sequence is incidental. The first part of the number indicates the number of the Congress (*e.g.* "P.L. 96–15" is public law number 15 of the 96th Congress). Illustration 5b indicates the various parts of an enactment.

   You should also check your own state's session laws in the law library. The enactments from each year or session will be collected, numbered, and printed in a series of volumes going back to your state's beginning. From state to state the titles of these series will vary *e.g.: Statutes and Amendments to the Codes, Laws of the State of . . . , Public and Local Acts of . . . , Session Laws, Acts and Resolves of . . . , General and Special Laws,* etc.[21] Each enactment is given a consecutive number. Most states call them "act numbers," or simply "numbers." One major state (Ohio) continues to use the original bill number, even after they are signed into law.

---

20. Private laws provide relief for named individuals who have suffered certain wrongs at the hands of the government. Reorganization plans are Presidential proposals to establish, abolish, or reorganize government agencies. They are submitted for Congressional approval. You are probably already familiar with Congressional resolutions and Presidential proclamations.

21. As noted these are all "session laws." Learn to recognize law books by the contents and arrangement on the inside. The titles on the cover are often uninformative, if not actually misleading.

Session laws are primary material and are the first official publication of an enactment.[22] As you will learn next, however, they are not particularly useful for research and your initial inclination should be to look for a set of law books which *compiles* statutory law. This research tool is called an "annotated code."

Correct Citation Form for Session Laws

Federal

Sugar Act Amendment of 1971, Pub. L. No. 92–138, §3, 85 Stat. 379

State

Ch. 867, §1, [1945] Cal. Stat. 1626

---

22. Some states initially publish their enactments as individual pamphlets before they are bound together. These pamphlets are called "slip laws." The promptest publication of session laws, at least for the larger states, is the "legislative service," "session law service," "current legislation" or service by similar name that accompanies the state's annotated code. See p. 72.

Illustrations 5a and 5b. A Session Law.

UNITED STATES
STATUTES AT LARGE

CONTAINING THE

LAWS AND CONCURRENT RESOLUTIONS
ENACTED DURING THE FIRST SESSION OF THE
NINETY-SIXTH CONGRESS
OF THE UNITED STATES OF AMERICA

1979

AND

REORGANIZATION PLANS
AND PROCLAMATIONS

VOLUME 93

IN ONE PART

UNITED STATES
GOVERNMENT PRINTING OFFICE
WASHINGTON : 1981

Illustration 5a. Title page from Volume 93 *United States Statutes at Large.*

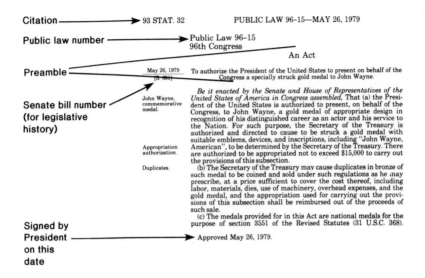

Citation ————————➤ 93 STAT. 32   PUBLIC LAW 96-15—MAY 26, 1979

Public law number ————————➤ Public Law 96-15
96th Congress

An Act

Preamble —————   May 26, 1979   To authorize the President of the United States to present on behalf of the
[S. 631]   Congress a specially struck gold medal to John Wayne.

Be it enacted by the Senate and House of Representatives of the
United States of America in Congress assembled, That (a) the Presi-
Senate bill number ————   John Wayne,   dent of the United States is authorized to present, on behalf of the
(for legislative   commemorative   Congress, to John Wayne, a gold medal of appropriate design in
medal.   recognition of his distinguished career as an actor and his service to
history)   the Nation. For such purpose, the Secretary of the Treasury is
authorized and directed to cause to be struck a gold medal with
suitable emblems, devices, and inscriptions, including "John Wayne,
Appropriation   American", to be determined by the Secretary of the Treasury. There
authorization.   are authorized to be appropriated not to exceed $15,000 to carry out
the provisions of this subsection.
Duplicates.   (b) The Secretary of the Treasury may cause duplicates in bronze of
such medal to be coined and sold under such regulations as he may
prescribe, at a price sufficient to cover the cost thereof, including
labor, materials, dies, use of machinery, overhead expenses, and the
gold medal, and the appropriation used for carrying out the provisions of this subsection shall be reimbursed out of the proceeds of
such sale.
(c) The medals provided for in this Act are national medals for the
Signed by   purpose of section 3551 of the Revised Statutes (31 U.S.C. 368).
President ————————➤ Approved May 26, 1979.
on this
date

Legislative
history   LEGISLATIVE HISTORY:
document   SENATE REPORT No. 96-110 (Comm. on Banking, Housing, and Urban Affairs).
    CONGRESSIONAL RECORD, Vol. 125 (1979):
citations   May 3, considered and passed Senate.
      May 23, H.R. 3767 considered and passed House; passage vacated and S. 631,
for Senate   amended, passed in lieu; Senate concurred in House amendment.
    WEEKLY COMPILATION OF PRESIDENTIAL DOCUMENTS, Vol. 15, No. 22:
bill 631   May 26, Presidential statement.

Illustration 5b. From Volume 93 *United States Statutes at Large.*

B. Annotated Codes[23]—What Do They Do?

Perhaps the best way to understand annotated codes is to imagine how you would research statutory law if such books did not exist. Take your own state's statutes as an example and let us say that you wanted to find the current state requirements for child adoption. You would have to start with the latest volume of the session laws and then look at every other volume back to your state's founding. Only in this way would you be sure to have the texts of all the related statutes on your subject, along with their amendments and repeals. Next you would compare the texts, do some cutting and pasting, and then you would have the current "law in force." Your final step would be to search through all of your state's case law to see what the courts have said, if anything, on how this statutory law is to be interpreted and applied.

Having endured this drudgery, it would become apparent that there was a need for a set of books that:

(1) arranged all of the statutes by subject,
(2) deleted the repealed portions and inserted the amendments and additions,
(3) provided a general index,
(4) was supplemented frequently, and
(5) cited cases that had considered any of the statutes.

That is what annotated codes do.[24]

1. The Arrangement of Annotated Codes

Annotated codes are arranged by subject. All of the legislation of a jurisdiction is organized under such headings as agriculture, taxation, vehicles, civil procedure, education, etc. (See Illustration 7a.)

You can generally get an overview of your state's arrangement by glancing at the information on the book spines as the set sits on the shelf. With the federal codes, these subjects are given a title number that is

---

23. This legal tool will be called "annotated codes" (or simply, "the set"). Annotated codes are essentially the same from state to state, but go under varying names, including: "Code," "Revised Code," "Annotated Statutes," "Statutes," "Revised Statutes," "General Statutes," "Consolidated Statutes," "General Laws," "Consolidated Laws," "and Compiled Laws." There are theoretical distinctions between codifications, revisions, consolidations, and compilations, but these distinctions are seldom observed rigorously. You should use the term that is current in your state. See M. Price, H. Bitner, and S. Bysiewicz, *Effective Legal Research* 29 and 30 (4th ed. 1979) for the technical definitions. In any case, do not confuse the subject arranged annotated codes with the chronologically arranged session laws.

24. The following parts provide an overall explanation of the five features listed above. Further detail on some of these features, however, has been left for "The Steps in Using Annotated Codes" on p. 69 et seq.

ultimately divided into sections (Illustrations 7c and 7d); some states do the same. Another common method is simply to number in continuous section numbers from the beginning to the end of the entire set. Other states will go title to chapter or chapter to section. In California, New York, and other states, the codes are labeled by name of subject matter and section. (*E.g.* Cal. Penal Code § 1243; N.Y. Educ. Law § 2585)

2. Annotated Codes Provide the Text of the Statutes in Force.

As indicated earlier, the compilers of annotated codes go into that immense body of legislation produced throughout the history of a jurisdiction, and extract what is still in force. It is a kind of cutting and pasting task. Your state's original child adoption statute may have been enacted over a hundred years ago but, during its history, chapters, sections, sentences, phrases, or even single words may have been deleted, or modified, or added to it. An annotated code does all this in order to give you the text of the law as it stands today.

3. Getting into Annotated Codes: Index and Analytic Approaches

All annotated codes have a general index to the entire set. Often there are also separate indexes for individual volumes or parts. The index will be your primary method of getting into the annotated statutes. Illustrations 6a–6m show a sample search in an annotated code using the index approach.

Another approach is the "analytic approach." Annotated codes have tables preceding the various parts of the set. These tables set forth the arrangement of the statutes. They go under various names, such as: "Analysis," "Table of Contents," "Table of Chapters," "Table of Titles and Chapters," etc. Generally several different tables are provided so that you can descend from the general to the specific. For instance, you might go from a

Table of Titles (for the entire set)

down to a

Table of Chapters (for each title)

down to a

Table of Sections (for each chapter)

Some state annotated codes provide you with a "Condensed Analysis" which is followed by a detailed "Analysis." These provide a kind of table of contents to major subject areas in the statutes.

Illustrations 7a–7e show a sample search in an annotated code using the analytic approach.

4. **Supplementation of Annotated Codes**

Needless to say, there is enough new legislation coming down during each year to make prompt supplementation a necessary feature of annotated codes.

The most common method of supplementation is:

bound volume

to

pocket part

to

pamphlets (two kinds)

Under this method there are pocket parts in the back of each bound volume which bring the bound volumes up to date from the time the bound volumes were published to the end of the prior year. (*E.g.* 1985 pocket parts cover through December 31, 1984.) The pocket parts have the same arrangement and numbering as their bound volumes.

The pocket parts are then further supplemented by what the publishers call "pamphlets." They come out periodically during the current year and are shelved at the end of the set. These pamphlets (which look more like booklets) are of two kinds: annotation service and legislative service.

The annotation service provides annotations from the current year.[25] It is arranged and numbered like the set itself and serves as a direct supplement to the pocket parts. These annotation service pamphlets are generally called "cumulative pamphlets" or "interim annotation service." The legislative service provides you with this year's statutes in session law form.

In addition to the regular pattern of bound volume to pocket part to pamphlets (annotation and legislative services), you may also encounter a further wrinkle. When a pocket part becomes too large, as new material is added year after year, the publisher will ordinarily come out with a "replacement volume." This will be a completely new bound volume that incorporates everything in the old bound volume and its pocket part. Sometimes, however, the publisher will not immediately come out with a replacement volume. Instead, a booklet will be produced that will sit on the shelf next to the bound volume it supplements. Generally the booklet will have a statement on its cover that reads something like: "Vol. 22 interim supplement—for use with main volume."

---

25. A few sets, notably the *United States Code Annotated* (U.S.C.A.) and the *United States Code Service* (U.S.C.S.), supplement the statutory text as well as the annotations in the same pamphlets.

A few state annotated codes are in looseleaf form or, at least, use a designated "current" looseleaf volume/s for supplementation. Looseleaf sets are supplemented by the issuance of new pages that contain the latest revisions, additions, etc. The library staff inserts these new pages and discards the old pages. The advantage of looseleaf supplementation is that you only have to look in one place.

If you had trouble following these last few paragraphs, remember what was said about going into a law library and looking at the books *in situ.*

5. The Annotations in Annotated Codes[26]

Annotated codes are fairly uniform in the type of annotations they provide. Annotations are typically set forth in the following order:

a. **Sources Note**

Immediately after the statutory text—often in parentheses and without a heading—you find citations to the session law sources of that text.

b. **History Note**

This note cites prior statutes and perhaps quotes earlier language to show how the text was modified over the years.

c. **References to Administrative Regulations**

The two federal sets, for example, give you citations to the *U.S. Code of Federal Regulations* (C.F.R.).

d. **Cross References**

These are citations to related sections in the annotated codes.

e. **References to other Publications**

Under headings like "Library Reference," "Research Guide," or "Collateral Reference"—annotated codes provide citations to formbooks, legal encyclopedias, annotated reporters, textbooks, looseleaf services or other commentaries[27] on the topic in question. Not surprisingly, publishers tend to favor their own "other publications."

f. **References to Law Reviews**

These are citations to law review articles on the topic.

g. **Notes of Decisions**

These are digests of language from court opinions which have cited the section of the statutes in question. Attorney general

---

26. The sources cited in the annotations (reporters, form books, administrative codes, attorney general opinions, and commentaries) are all covered as separate topics elsewhere in this work.

27. Incidentally, when you are unfamiliar with an area of the law, it is generally more efficient to start your research with the commentaries. (See Section 3.)

opinions are sometimes included here, when they are not under their own heading.[28]

h. **Other Notes**

Additional notes that are sometimes found include: "Practice Reminders," "Law Revision Comments," "Legislative Committee Comments," and anything else the publishers feel is relevant. Some sets will even include extensive signed articles by experts on newly enacted codes or revisions of the statutes.

Illustration 7e shows most of the types of annotations covered above.

6. **Parallel Sets of Annotated Codes**

The federal government and a few states have more than one set of their statutory codes. This occurs because there may be one set published by the government as well as one by a private publisher—or there may be competing private publishers. Most of the governmental sets are not particularly useful. They have few or no annotations[29] and, as with all government publications, they are notoriously late in publishing. Of course, only the government sets contain the official text. But, the commercially published sets have such a reputation for accuracy and are so widely used that the distinction between official and unofficial is academic.

At the federal level, there are three sets of statutory codes:

(1) *United States Code* (U.S.C.): An official publication of the United States Government. It is not annotated.

(2) *United States Code Annotated* (U.S.C.A.): Published by West Publishing Co. (hereinafter "West").

(3) *United States Code Service* (U.S.C.S.): Published by Lawyers Co-Operative/Bancroft Whitney Publishing companies (hereinafter "Lawyers Co-Op").

All three federal sets use the same numbering system. For example, if you were in the military and wished to know your worth in terms of square feet of floor space, you would want to consult the following federal statute:[30]

---

28. The attorney general is the government's lawyer. One of his or her functions is to provide written opinions on questions of law submitted by government officials (legislators, chiefs of agencies, district attorneys, county counsels, etc.). These published opinions are recognized by the courts as strong persuasive authority.

29. An unannotated code can be handy, however, when you are only interested in the statutory text, particularly if it is extensive. For example, the Internal Revenue Code fits into a small volume, but the annotated version in U.S.C.A. requires sixteen volumes.

30. In legal writing, note that a quotation exceeding three lines is blocked off (as illustrated) and omits quotation marks. Also note the use of ellipses to indicate omissions and brackets to indicate additions.

In the construction of family quarters for members of the Armed Forces, the following are the maximum space limitations:

Pay Grade . . .	Net floor area (square feet)
0–7 [Generals]	2,100
0–6 [Colonels]	1,700
0–4 and 0–5 [Majors and Lt. Colonels]	1,550
0–1 through 0–3 [Officers below Major]	1,450
. . .	
E–1 through E–6 [Enlisted members]	1,350

. . .

The various citations for the above statute are:

10 U.S.C. §2684(a) (1976)
10 U.S.C.A. §2684(a) (1975)
10 U.S.C.S. §2684(a) (1979)

The dates in parentheses indicate the date of publication or copyright of the particular volume in which title 10, section 2684 (a) was found at the time it was cited.[31] The "Blue Book" rule is that you cite only to the official U.S.C. when the statute can be found there. Since U.S.C. is not supplemented as rapidly as the commercial sets, you may have to cite them for recent legislation.

Correct Citation Form for Codes

Federal
    31 U.S.C. §691 (1970).
State
    Cal. Civ. Pro. Code §437c (West, 1954).

III. Steps in Using Annotated Codes (Index Approach)

Step 1. State the issue.

Let us say that you are a Sierra Club type and you want Congress to declare a Scenic Trail that would run from Dead Horse Creek to Carson Sink Nevada. You are quick to perceive that, at first blush, such a route does not sound all that scenic. The issue is: National Scenic Trails embrace what types of natural areas?

---

31. The acid test for all citations is: Can someone find the same book and page you have in your hand—ten years later and a thousand miles away? The date, therefore, of any volume or supplement you are using should be part of the citation.

Step 2. Find the set of annotated code for the jurisdiction in question.
This is obviously a federal problem so we will turn to one of the federal annotated codes. For this example we will use the *United States Code Service.* Illustrations 6a–6m reproduce sample pages from the volumes of U.S.C.S. you would use in solving this problem.

Step 3. Go to the index.
Using law book indexes is likely to be one of your more frustrating experiences in legal research. Your difficulty will be to guess how the compiler indexed the material you are looking for. One thing to keep in mind is that everyday factual words as well as legal terms are used.

In our illustrative problem we find an index entry that reads:

> National Trails System
> Composition, 16 §1242

(See Illustration 6b)

Step 4. Go to the referenced title and section.
In our illustration we are referred to title 16, section 1242 of the U.S.C.S. If you turn to that section (Illustration 6d) you first see a heading in bold face that starts out: "Composition of national trails system . . ." This heading was merely made up by the compiler, but all of the language after that heading down to the source note, *viz.* "(Oct. 2, 1968, P.L. 90–543 . . .)", is *the text of the law.* It is word-for-word the same language that was enacted into law by Congress. You could prove this to yourself by getting the citation from the source note and going to *U.S. Statutes at Large* to find the original statute in session law form.

Step 5. Read the text of the law carefully.
Statutory language is very deliberate: each word counts. Approach it as you would reading a question on an examination. What does the statute say, *precisely*? Are there any ambiguities in the text that can help or hurt your client? The public calls this "looking for loopholes," but lawyers like to call it "statutory construction."

In our problem we can see in paragraph (b) of §1242 that National Scenic Trails are composed of locations that:

> [P]rovide for maximum outdoor recreation potential and for the conversation and enjoyment of the national significant scenic, historic, natural or cultural qualities of the areas . . .

The key phrase for our problem would seem to be "national significant scenic . . . or natural . . . area". Does that include all

that alkali dust and creosote bush that lies between Dead Horse
Creek and Carson Sink?

Step 6. Read the annotations.

In our problem we only find one so far and that is citation to the
federal regulation that was promulgated under this section of the
statute. If you checked in CFR you would find that it does not help
us on our problem. The most important type of annotations are
headnotes from court opinions[32] but there are none in this problem.

Step 7. Check the pocket part.

If you look at the copyright date of any volume in a set of annotated codes, you will generally find that it was published several
years ago. Obviously, the publishers have supplemented that
volume, since the user needs to know the current law. Most annotated codes are supplemented by pocket parts. They come out
annually and are inserted into a pocket located inside the back
cover.

The pocket part uses the same numbering system as the bound
volume, therefore you can check your original reference number
(title and section, code and section, etc.) there.

The pocket part will tell you if the language of the statute
you have read in the bound volume has been affected by subsequent amendments, repeals, etc. It also updates the annotations.
Generally, it supplements the bound volume through December of
the prior year.[33]

In our problem (see Illustrations 6f and 6g), we see that subsections (c) and (d) were added and redesignated, but neither this
nor the new CFR annotations help us.

---

32. The courts have a fair measure of discretion in interpreting the text and determining
the constitutionality of statutes. Therefore, you will want to read cases similar to yours
which have applied the section of the codes in question.

   If you want to see a quick example of how important court interpretations can
be, turn to 26 U.S.C.S. §61. There, under the law that defines income for tax purposes,
you have twenty lines of statutory language and 165 pages of case annotations from
over a thousand cases. These case annotations (also called digests, headnotes, squibs
or syllabi) are abstracts of discussions of points of law in cases that have cited §61.
The abstract is followed by a citation to the case from which it comes. The origin of
these is explained more fully on p. 36.

33. The trick to updating all legal research is to check the dates of coverage of any bound
volume, pocket part, booklet, pamphlet, or looseleaf page you are using. Look for
statements like: "For use in 1985," or "This pamphlet supplements the pocket parts
for use in 1985," or "Legislation through Chapter 451," etc. If you read such statements and carefully look around on the shelves nearby for all parts of the set, your
research should be up to date.

Step 8. Check the Annotations Pamphlet.

The pocket part brings you up through the end of the prior year. During the current year, for most states, publishers issue soft bound booklets that are typically called: "Cumulative Pamphlets" or "Later Case Service". They update the case and other annotations in the bound volumes and pocket parts.[34]

As noted earlier, on the federal level there are two competing annotated code services: West's *United States Code Annotated* and Lawyers Co-Op's *United States Code Service.* Both sets have annotations pamphlets. In U.S.C.A. they are just called "Pamphlet number 1, 2, 3, etc. In U.S.C.S. they are called "Cumulative Later Case and Statutory Service." Like all annotation pamphlets, state or federal, they directly supplement the pocket parts and therefore are arranged by the same titles and sections as the main body of the set.

Getting back to our problem, Illustrations 6h–6j are reproduced from the annotations pamphlet in U.S.C.S. As you can see, there were no new entries under 16 U.S.C.S. §1242. Although there are none in our problem, Illustration 6j gives some examples of case annotations.

Step 9. Check the Legislative Service.

The legislative service gives you the text of new session laws as they are passed by the legislature.[35] It comes out frequently when the legislature is in session. Each issue contains a table with a title like: "Table of sections amended, repealed, added, etc." *This is the first place you go to when using a legislative service.* The table is cumulative, so always go to the latest issue for the current year. Look under your annotated code reference (title and section, code and section, etc.) and the table will refer you to the appropriate page in the legislative service where you will find the text of the new session law that affects your section of the annotated code.

The legislative service in U.S.C.A. is called *U.S. Code: Congressional and Administrative News.* In addition to containing the current session laws, this service also provides the text of certain documents used for a legislative history (see pp. 98–103).

---

34. The advance sheets of the case reporters (see page 23) have tables of "Statutes Construed." The advance sheets may be more recent than the annotation supplements.

35. The "annotations pamphlets" for both federal annotated codes also update the statutory text to some extent, but you must take Step 9 anyhow because the annotations pamphlets do not come out as frequently as the legislative service.

The legislative service in U.S.C.S. is simply called "Advance". In our problem, illustrations 6k–6m are reproduced from pages in that service. The first place we check is the latest cumulative "Table of Code Sections Added, Amended, Repealed, or Otherwise Affected." In Illustration 6l we see that title 16, section 1242(b) was amended by Public Law 98–11. When we read the text of that session law in the legislative service (Illustration 6m), we see the added language: "Natural scenic trails may be located so as to represent desert . . . areas" Since Congress has now specifically included desert locations within the Scenic Trails system—the Dead Horse to Carson sink project gains new life.

Step 10. Further updating?

The preceding nine steps constitute a complete search for statutory law, at least for ordinary purposes. In extraordinary circumstances, further updating can be done by consulting a newsletter or other service that reports on legislative activities, if one exists for your jurisdiction. Newspapers are another source of information. The librarian in a library documents department will also be of help.

Illustrations 6a–6m. Steps in Using Annotated Codes (Index Approach).

Step 1:
State the
issue—
"National Scenic
Trails embrace
what types of
natural areas?"

Step 2:
Find the
annotated
code for the
jurisdiction
in question.

All federal laws of a general and permanent nature arranged in accordance with
the section numbering of the United
States Code and the supplements
thereto.

Step 3:
Go to the index. ─────────➤ **General Index**

N-R

1973

THE LAWYERS CO-OPERATIVE PUBLISHING CO.
Rochester, New York 14603

BANCROFT-WHITNEY CO.
San Francisco, California 94107

Illustration 6a. Title page from General Index N–R of the *United States Code Service*, Lawyers Edition. Copyright © 1973 by the Lawyers Co-Operative Publishing Company / Bancroft-Whitney Company. Reprinted with permission.

UNITED STATES CODE SERVICE

NATL SERVICE LIFE INS.—Cont'd
Witnesses, actions, 38 § 784

NATIONAL SHRINE
General Grant Tree, 16 § 80a note

NATIONAL SICKLE CELL ANEMIA CONTROL ACT
Generally, 42 §§ 300b–300b-5
Program authorized, 42 §§ 300b–300b-5

NATIONAL SPACE PROGRAM
Aeronautics and Space (this index)

NATIONAL STATUARY HALL
Arrangement and use, 40 § 187
Art exhibit in hall prohibited, 40 § 189
Creation, 40 § 187

NATIONAL STOLEN PROPERTY ACT
Generally, 18 §§ 10, 2311, 2314, 2315, 3237

NATIONAL SYMBOL
Bald Eagle (this index)

NATIONAL SYSTEM OF INTERSTATE AND DEFENSE HIGHWAYS
Highways (this index)

NATIONAL TECHNICAL INSTITUTE FOR THE DEAF ACT
Generally, 20 § 681 et seq.
Deaf Persons (this index)
Short title, 20 § 681 note

NATIONAL TOURISM RESOURCES REVIEW COMMISSION
Establishment, composition, functions, etc., 22 § 2121 note

NATIONAL TRAFFIC AND MOTOR VEHICLE SAFETY ACT OF 1966
Generally, 15 §§ 1381 note, 1391–1409, 1421–1426, 1431; 23 § 313 note
Motor Vehicles (this index)

NATIONAL TRAFFIC SAFETY BUREAU
Compensation, Director, 5 § 5316
Director
– appointment, etc., 49 § 1652
– compensation, 5 § 5316
– head of Bureau, 49 § 1652
Establishment, 49 § 1652
National Traffic and Motor Vehicle Safety Act, carrying out provisions, 15 § 1404; 49 § 1652

NATIONAL TRAILS SYSTEM
Generally, 16 § 1241 et seq.
Acquisition of lands within exterior boundaries of areas included in rights-of-way, 16 § 1246

130

Acreage limitation, acquisition of lands within exterior boundaries of areas included in right-of-way, 16 § 1246
Act of Congress necessary, relocation, scenic trail rights-of-way, 16 § 1246
Additional scenic trails, 16 § 1244
Administration of scenic trails, 16 §§ 1244, 1246
Advisory councils for scenic trails, establishment, duties, etc., 16 § 1244
Agreement, federal officials having jurisdiction over selected lands, rights-of-way for scenic trails, 16 § 1246
Appalachian Trail
– appropriations, acquisition of lands or interests therein, 16 § 1249
– component of, 16 § 1241
– establishment, description, administration, etc., 16 § 1244
– relocation and reconstruction of portions disturbed by Blue Ridge Parkway extension, 16 § 460a-7
Appropriations, acquisition of lands or interests therein for scenic trails, 16 § 1249
Composition, 16 § 1242
Concurrence, heads of federal agencies, regulations governing use, protection, etc., 16 § 1246
Condemnation proceedings to acquire private lands, 16 § 1246
Conditions in easements and rights-of-way, 16 § 1248
Congressional declaration of policy, 16 § 1241
Connecting or side trails
– establishment, designation, and marking as components of System, 16 § 1245
– part of System, 16 § 1242
Consent
– agencies, etc., connecting or side trails, location, 16 § 1245
– federal agencies, etc., establishment, recreation trails, 16 § 1243
Consultation
– additional scenic trails, 16 § 1244
– administration, Appalachian Trail, 16 § 1244
– advisory councils for scenic trails, 16 § 1244
– establishment, uniform markers, 16 § 1242
– regulations, use, protection, etc., 16 § 1246
Cooperation
– agencies, etc., additional scenic trails, 16 § 1244
– federal agencies with Secretaries of Interior and Agriculture, 16 § 1248
– states over portions of recreation or scenic trails located outside of federally administered areas, development and maintenance, 16 § 1246

References are to Titles and Sections

Subheading—
(Refers to title 16, section 1242 of U.S.C.S.)

Heading—————————▶

Illustration 6b. Page 130 from General Index N–R of the *United States Code Service,* Lawyers Edition. Copyright © 1973 by the Lawyers Co-Operative Publishing Company / Bancroft-Whitney Company. Reprinted with permission.

All federal laws of a general and permanent nature arranged in accordance with
the section numbering of the United
States Code and the supplements
thereto.

Step 4:
Go to the
referenced title ————————————**16 USCS**
Conservation

§§ 831–END
Index

1978

THE LAWYERS CO-OPERATIVE PUBLISHING CO.
Rochester, New York 14603

BANCROFT-WHITNEY CO.
San Francisco, California 94107

Illustration 6c. Title page from last volume of Title 16 of the *United States Code Service*, Lawyers Edition. Copyright © 1978 by the Lawyers Co-Operative Publishing Company / Bancroft-Whitney Company. Reprinted with permission.

1247. State and local area recreation trails
    (a) Secretary of the Interior to encourage states, political subdivisions, and private interests; financial assistance for state and local projects
    (b) Secretary of Housing and Urban Development to encourage metropolitan and other urban areas; administrative and financial assistance in connection with recreation and transportation planning; administration of urban open-space program
    (c) Secretary of Agriculture to encourage states, local agencies, and private interests
    (d) Designation and marking of trails; approval of Secretary of the Interior
1248. Easements and rights-of-way; conditions; cooperation of federal agencies with Secretary of the Interior and Secretary of Agriculture
1249. Authorization of appropriations

---

§ 1241. National trails system; establishment; Congressional declaration of policy; initial components

(a) In order to provide for the ever-increasing outdoor recreation needs of an expanding population and in order to promote public access to, travel within, and enjoyment and appreciation of the open-air, outdoor areas of the Nation, trails should be established (i) primarily, near the urban areas of the Nation, and (ii) secondarily, within established scenic areas more remotely located.

(b) The purpose of this Act [16 USCS §§ 1241 et seq.] is to provide the means for attaining these objectives by instituting a national system of recreation and scenic trails, by designating the Appalachian Trail and the Pacific Crest Trail as the initial components of that system, and by prescribing the methods by which, and standards according to which, additional components may be added to the system.
(Oct. 2, 1968, P. L. 90-543, § 2, 82 Stat. 919.)

Step 4:
(continued)
Go to the
referenced
section.

HISTORY; ANCILLARY LAWS AND DIRECTIVES

Short titles:
Act Oct. 2, 1968, P. L. 90-543, § 1, 82 Stat. 919, provided: "This Act may be cited as the 'National Trails System Act'.". For full classification of this Act, consult USCS Tables volumes.

CODE OF FEDERAL REGULATIONS
36 CFR Part 251

Text of the
session law
begins here.

§ 1242. Composition of national trails system; recreation trails; scenic trails; connecting or side trails; uniform marker

The national system of trails shall be composed of—

352

Illustration 6d. Page 352 from the last volume of Title 16 of the *United States Code Service,* Lawyers Edition. Copyright © 1978 by the Lawyers Co-Operative Publishing Company/Bancroft-Whitney Company. Reprinted with permission.

Step 5:
Read the text
of the law

Text of the
session law

Source note
*(Statutes at
Large)* ———▶

Step 6:
Read the
annotations

NATIONAL TRAILS SYSTEM   **16 USCS § 1243**

(a) National recreation trails, established as provided in section 4 of this
Act [16 USCS § 1243], which will provide a variety of outdoor recreation uses in or reasonably accessible to urban areas.

(b) National scenic trails, established as provided in section 5 of this Act
[16 USCS § 1244], which will be extended trails so located as to provide
for maximum outdoor recreation potential and for the conservation and
enjoyment of the national significant scenic, historic, natural, or cultural
qualities of the areas through which such trails may pass.

(c) Connecting or side trails, established as provided in section 6 of this
Act [16 USCS § 1245], which will provide additional points of public
access to national recreation or national scenic trails or which will
provide connections between such trails.

The Secretary of the Interior and the Secretary of Agriculture, in consultation with appropriate governmental agencies and public and private organizations, shall establish a uniform marker for the national trails system.
(Oct. 2, 1968, P. L. 90-543, § 3, 82 Stat. 919.)

CODE OF FEDERAL REGULATIONS

36 CFR Part 251

**§ 1243. National recreation trails; establishment and designation;
prerequisites**

(a) The Secretary of the Interior, or the Secretary of Agriculture where
lands administered by him are involved, may establish and designate
national recreation trails, with the consent of the Federal agency, State, or
political subdivision having jurisdiction over the lands involved, upon
finding that—

(i) such trails are reasonably accessible to urban areas, and, or

(ii) such trails meet the criteria established in this Act [16 USCS §§ 1241
et seq.] and such supplementary criteria as he may prescribe.

(b) As provided in this section, trails within park, forest, and other
recreation areas administered by the Secretary of the Interior or the
Secretary of Agriculture or in other federally administered areas may be
established and designated as "National Recreation Trails" by the appropriate Secretary and, when no Federal land acquisition is involved—

(i) trails in or reasonably accessible to urban areas may be designated as
"National Recreation Trails" by the Secretary of the Interior with the
consent of the States, their political subdivisions, or other appropriate
administering agencies, and

(ii) trails within park, forest, and other recreation areas owned or
administered by States may be designated as "National Recreation
Trails" by the Secretary of the Interior with the consent of the State.
(Oct. 2, 1968, P. L. 90-543, § 4, 82 Stat. 919.)

353

Illustration 6e. Page 353 from the last volume of Title 16 of the *United
States Code Service,* Lawyers Edition. Copyright © 1978 by the Lawyers
Co-Operative Publishing Company/Bancroft-Whitney Company. Reprinted
with permission.

★ ★ ★ ★ ★ ★ ★ ★ ★ ★

UNITED STATES CODE SERVICE

Lawyers Edition

Step 7:
Check the
pocket part

Issued in

May, 1983

CUMULATIVE SUPPLEMENT

By The Publisher's Editorial Staff

16 USCS
Conservation
§§ 831–End

THE LAWYERS CO-OPERATIVE PUBLISHING CO.
Rochester, New York 14694

BANCROFT-WHITNEY CO.
San Francisco, California 94107

LCP BW

Pkg # 33

Illustration 6f. May 1983 pocket part from last volume of Title 16 of the *United States Code Service*, Lawyers Edition. Copyright © 1983 by the Lawyers Co-Operative Publishing Company / Bancroft-Whitney Company. Reprinted with permission.

Step 7: (continued) Check the pocket part

HISTORY: ANCILLARY LAWS AND DIRECTIVES

Amendments:
1978. Act Nov. 10, 1978, in subsec. (a), added "the preservation of,", added "and historic resources", substituted new clause (ii), exclusive of subsequent amendments, for one which read: "secondarily, within established scenic areas more remotely located."; in subsec. (b), substituted ", scenic and historic" for "and scenic".

CODE OF FEDERAL REGULATIONS

Add:
36 CFR Part 212.
43 CFR Part 8000.
43 CFR Part 8300.
43 CFR Part 8350.
43 CFR Part 8370.
43 CFR Part 9260.

§ 1242. Composition of national trails system; recreation trails; scenic trails; historic trails; connecting or side trails; uniform marker

[Introductory matter unchanged]

(a), (b) [Unchanged]

Congress added to § 1242 in 1978

(c) National historic trails, established as provided in section 5 of this Act [16 USCS § 1244], which will be extended trails which follow as closely as possible and practicable the original trails or routes of travel of national historical significance. Designation of such trails or routes shall be continuous, but the established or developed trail, and the acquisition thereof, need not be continuous onsite. National historic trails shall have as their purpose the identification and protection of the historic route and its historic remnants and artifacts for public use and enjoyment. Only those selected land and water based components of an historic trail which are on federally owned lands and which meet the national historic trail criteria established in this Act [16 USCS §§ 1241 et seq.], are established as initial Federal protection components of a national historic trail. The appropriate Secretary may subsequently certify other lands as protected segments of an historic trail upon application from State or local governmental agencies or private interests involved if such segments meet the national historic trail criteria established in this Act [16 USCS §§ 1241 et seq.] and such criteria supplementary thereto as the appropriate Secretary may prescribe, and are administered by such agencies or interests without expense to the United States.

(d) Connecting or side trails, established as provided in section 6 of this Act [16 USCS § 1245], which will provide additional points of public access to national recreation, national scenic or national historic trails or which will provide connections between such trails.

[Concluding matter unchanged]

(As amended Nov. 10, 1978, P. L. 95-625, Title V, Subtitle B, § 551(4), (5), 92 Stat. 3511.)

HISTORY: ANCILLARY LAWS AND DIRECTIVES

Amendments:
1978. Act Nov. 10, 1978, redesignated subsec. (c) as subsec. (d), added new subsec. (c); in subsec. (d), as redesignated, substituted ", national scenic or national historic" for "or national scenic".

more annotations

CODE OF FEDERAL REGULATIONS

Add:
36 CFR Part 212.
43 CFR Part 8000.
43 CFR Part 8370.
43 CFR Part 9260.

§ 1243   National recreation trails; establishment and designation; prerequisites

CODE OF FEDERAL REGULATIONS

Add:
36 CFR Part 212.
43 CFR Part 8000.
43 CFR Part 8370.
43 CFR Part 9260.

§ 1244.   National scenic and national historic trails

(a) Establishment and designation of various national scenic and historic trails; administration; exceptions to prohibition on use of motorized vehicles. National scenic and national historic trails shall be authorized and designated only by Act of Congress. There are hereby established the following National Scenic and National Historic Trails:

(1) The Appalachian National Scenic Trail, a trail of approximately two thousand miles extending generally along the Appalachian Mountains from Mount Katahdin, Maine, to Springer Mountain, Georgia. Insofar as practicable, the right-of-way for such trail shall comprise the trail depicted on the maps identified as "Nationwide System of Trails, Proposed Appalachian Trails, NST-AT-101-May 1967", which shall be on file and available for public inspection in the office of the Director of the National Park Service. Where practicable, such rights-of-way shall include lands protected for it under agreements in effect as of the date of enactment of this Act [enacted Oct. 2, 1968], to which

Illustration 6g. Page 79 of May 1983 pocket part from last volume of Title 16 of the *United States Code Service*, Lawyers Edition. Copyright © 1983 by the Lawyers Co-Operative Publishing Company / Bancroft-Whitney Company. Reprinted with permission.

★ ★ ★ ★ ★ **UNITED STATES CODE SERVICE** *Lawyers Edition* ★ ★ ★ ★

Step 8:
Check the
annotations
pamphlet

June 1983

**CUMULATIVE
LATER CASE
and
STATUTORY SERVICE**

through Public Law 98–10

Supplementing 1983 Pocket Parts

Issued in
June 1983
By the Publisher's Editorial Staff

THE LAWYERS CO-OPERATIVE PUBLISHING CO.
Rochester, New York 14694

BANCROFT-WHITNEY CO.
San Francisco, California 94107

LCP BWD

Illustration 6h. Title page from June 1983 Cumulative Later Case and Statutory Service of the *United States Code Service,* Lawyers Edition. Copyright © 1983 by the Lawyers Co-Operative Publishing Company/Bancroft-Whitney Company. Reprinted with permission.

such project is required to obtain license from Commission, and obtain necessary right-of-way by method prescribed in § 8 of MIRA. Escondido

Mut. Water Co. v Federal Energy Regulatory Com. (1982, CA9) 692 F2d 1223.

§ 824. Declaration of policy; application of subchapter; definitions

INTERPRETIVE NOTES AND DECISIONS

5. Interstate electric energy transmission (16 USCS § 824(d))

FERC has exclusive jurisdiction, to exclusion of state public service commission, over agreement between electric utility companies to interconnect

their transmission systems since such agreement provides for transmission for resale of electric energy in interstate commerce. Utah v Federal Energy Regulatory Com. (1982, CA10) 691 F2d 444.

Step 8: (continued) Check the annotations pamphlet

§ 825. Accounts and records

INTERPRETIVE NOTES AND DECISIONS

16 USCS § 825s empowers Secretary of Energy to promulgate interim rates for sale of federal hydroelectric power, and Secretary is entitled, under § 825s and under Department of Energy Organization Act (42 USCS §§ 7101 et seq.) to employ trifurcated procedure in raising rates under contracts tracking § 825s under which (1) assistant

Secretary prepares new rate schedules, (2) another assistant Secretary is authorized to place such rates in effect on interim basis and (3) FERC is given final confirmation and approval authority. United States v Tex-La Electric Cooperative, Inc. (1982, CA5 La) 693 F2d 392.

CHAPTER 12A.   TENNESSEE VALLEY AUTHORITY

§ 831.   Creation; short title

RESEARCH GUIDE

Am Jur:
32 Am Jur 2d, Federal Employers' Liability and Compensation Acts, § 92.

CHAPTER 12G.   PACIFIC NORTHWEST FEDERAL TRANSMISSION SYSTEM

§ 839.   Purposes

INTERPRETIVE NOTES AND DECISIONS

District Court lacks jurisdiction to hear actions brought pursuant to NEPA (42 USCS §§ 4321 et seq.) challenging action of administrator of BPA in executing long-term power contracts which were entered into pursuant to Pacific Northwest Electric Power Planning and Conservation Act (16

USCS §§ 839 et seq.), since 16 USCS § 839f(e)(5) requires that such suits be brought in Court of Appeals rather than in District Court. National Wildlife Federation v Johnson (1982, DC Or) 548 F Supp 708.

(No entry for ──────▶ § 1242; *i.e.*, no changes or additions since pocket part.)

Illustration 6i. Page 285 from June 1983 Cumulative Later Case and Statutory Service of the *United States Code Service*, Lawyers Edition. Copyright © 1983 by the Lawyers Co-Operative Publishing Company / Bancroft-Whitney Company. Reprinted with permission.

16 USCS § 1382   USCS L ATER C ASE & S TATUTORY S ERVICE

CHAPTER 31.   MARINE MAMMAL PROTECTION

---

§ 1382.   Regulations and administration

CODE OF FEDERAL REGULATIONS

Add:
50 CFR Part 11.

CHAPTER 33.   COASTAL ZONE MANAGEMENT

---

§ 1456.   Coordination and cooperation

INTERPRETIVE NOTES AND DECISIONS

EPA acted arbitrarily in refusing to grant funds for construction of indispensable sewage treatment plant for proposed seaside community, after state granted permission for construction of dwelling units in community as exception to its general prohibition against floodplain development, since proposed development was fully in accord with state's management plan and Coastal Zone Management Act (42 USCS §§ 1451 et seq.). Cape May Greene, Inc. v Warren (1983, CA3 NJ) 698 F2d 179.

CHAPTER 35.   ENDANGERED SPECIES

Examples
of case
annotations

§ 1536.   Interagency cooperation

INTERPRETIVE NOTES AND DECISIONS

2. Injunctive relief
Action to compel Secretary to store water in reservoir for nearby municipal and industrial use will be dismissed since Secretary's plan of operating dam so as to restore species of lake fish to nonendangered status is supported by substantial evidence and since Secretary is required, under Endangered Species Act (16 USCS §§ 1531 et seq.) to give lake fish priority over all other purposes of dam until fish are no longer classified as endangered or threatened. Carson-Truckee Water Conservancy Dist. v Watt (1982, DC Nev) 549 F Supp 704.

§ 1540.   Penalties and enforcement

CODE OF FEDERAL REGULATIONS

Add:
50 CFR Part 11.

INTERPRETIVE NOTES AND DECISIONS

1. Civil penalties (16 USCS § 1540(a))
16 USCS § 1540(a)(1) does not impose strict liability upon commercial operators for totally innocent conduct; however, commercial operators are held to higher standard of conduct and will be liable for civil penalties if they knew or should have known that particular species was endangered; appeals board did not err in assessing $12,000 penalty against commercial operator who shipped 3 endangered turtles in violation of § 1540(a)(1). Newell v Baldridge (1982, WD Wash) 548 F Supp 39.

Illustration 6j. Page 286 from June 1983 Cumulative Later Case and Statutory Service of the *United States Code Service,* Lawyers Edition. Copyright © 1983 by the Lawyers Co-Operative Publishing Company / Bancroft-Whitney Company. Reprinted with permission.

ADVANCE

May, 1983
98th CONGRESS 1st SESSION

★ ★ ★ ★ ★ ★ ★ ★

**UNITED STATES
CODE SERVICE**

Lawyers Edition

Step 9:
Check the
legislative
service

Public Laws
98-8—98-20, pp. 3155-3206

Proposed Bankruptcy Rules
p. 3207

Federal Rules of Civil Procedure
Proposed Amendments, p. 3313
Federal Rules of Criminal Procedure
Proposed Amendments, p. 3337
Proclamations 5037-5054
pp. 3351-3385
Executive Orders 12413-12416
pp. 3387-3419
Administrative Regulations
pp. 3421-3440
Cumulative Index and Tables
pp. 3441-3555

LATE ITEMS—CURRENT
AWARENESS COMMENTARY

LCP BCO

Illustration 6k. Cover page of May 1983 "Advance" service from the
United States Code Service, Lawyers Edition. Copyright © 1983 by the
Lawyers Co-Operative Publishing Company / Bancroft-Whitney Company.
Reprinted with permission.

TABLE OF CODE SECTIONS ADDED, AMENDED, REPEALED,
OR OTHERWISE AFFECTED
98TH CONGRESS 1ST SESSION
(P. L. 98-1 -- 98-20)

	Section	Effect	Public Law No.
		TITLE 7	
Step 9: (continued) Check the legislative service	612c nt.	New	98-8 Title II, Sec. 201-210
		TITLE 15	
	313 nt.	New	98-8 Sec. 104
		TITLE 16	
	1241(b)	Amended	98-11 Sec. 202(1)
	1241(c)	Amended	98-11 Sec. 202(2)
	1241 nt.	New	98-11 Sec. 201
16 U.S.C.S. §1242(b) was amended by P.L. 98-11 ──────▶	1242(a)	Amended	98-11 Sec. 203(1)
	1242(a)(1)-(4)	Amended	98-11 Sec. 203(2)
	1242(a)(2)	Amended	98-11 Sec. 203(3)
	1242(a)(3)	Amended	98-11 Sec. 203(4),(5)
	1242(b),(c)	Amended	98-11 Sec. 203(6)
	1243(b)(i)	Amended	98-11 Sec. 204(2)
	1243(b)(i),(ii)	Amended	98-11 Sec. 204(1)
	1243(b)(ii)	Amended	98-11 Sec. 204(3)
	1243(b)(iii)	Amended	98-11 Sec. 204(4)
	1244(a)(11)-(13)	Amended	98-11 Sec. 205(a)
	1244(b)	Amended	98-11 Sec. 205(b)(1)
	1244(b)(3)	Amended	98-11 Sec. 205(b)(2)

3451

Illustration 6I. Page 3451 of May 1983 "Advance" service from the *United States Code Service,* Lawyers Edition. Copyright © 1983 by the Lawyers Co-Operative Publishing Company/Bancroft-Whitney Company. Reprinted with permission.

97 STAT. 42   PUBLIC LAW 98-11—MAR. 28, 1983

First page of the
text of P.L.
98-11

Public Law 98-11
98th Congress

An Act

Mar. 28, 1983
[S. 271]

To amend the National Trails System Act by designating additional national scenic and historic trails, and for other purposes.

Be it enacted by the Senate and House of Representatives of the United States of America in Congress assembled,

National Trails
System Act,
amendment.

TITLE I—LIMITATION ON APPROPRIATIONS

16 USC 1241
note.

SEC. 101. Authorizations of appropriations under this Act shall be effective only for the fiscal year beginning on October 1, 1983, and subsequent fiscal years. Notwithstanding any other provision of this Act, authority to enter into contracts, and to make payments, under this Act shall be effective only to such extent or in such amounts as are provided in advance in appropriation Acts.

National Trails
System Act
Amendments of
1983.
16 USC 1241
note.

TITLE II—AMENDMENTS TO THE NATIONAL TRAILS SYSTEM ACT

SEC. 201. This title may be cited as the "National Trails System Act Amendments of 1983".

SEC. 202. Section 2 of the National Trails System Act (82 Stat. 919; 16 U.S.C. 1241 et seq.) is amended—

(1) in subsection (b), by striking out "the purpose" and inserting in lieu thereof "The purpose"; and

(2) by adding at the end thereof the following new subsection:

"(c) The Congress recognizes the valuable contributions that volunteers and private, nonprofit trail groups have made to the development and maintenance of the Nation's trails. In recognition of these contributions, it is further the purpose of this Act to encourage and assist volunteer citizen involvement in the planning, development, maintenance, and management, where appropriate, of trails.".

16 USC 1242.

SEC. 203. Section 3 of the National Trails System Act is amended—

(1) by striking out "composed of—" and inserting in lieu thereof "composed of the following:";

(2) by redesignating paragraphs (a) through (d) as paragraphs (1) through (4), respectively, and by inserting "(a)" after "SEC. 3.";

National Scenic
Trails now
expressly
embrace
desert areas

(3) in paragraph (2) of subsection (a) (as so redesignated), by adding at the end thereof the following: "National scenic trails may be located so as to represent desert, marsh, grassland, mountain, canyon, river, forest, and other areas, as well as landforms which exhibit significant characteristics of the physiographic regions of the Nation.";

(4) in the fourth sentence of paragraph (3) of subsection (a) (as so redesignated), by striking out "Act, are established as initial" and inserting in lieu thereof "Act are included as";

Illustration 6m. Page 3184 of May 1983 "Advance" service from the *United States Code Service,* Lawyers Edition. Copyright © 1983 by the Lawyers Co-Operative Publishing Company/Bancroft-Whitney Company. Reprinted with permission.

IV. **Steps in Using Annotated Codes (Analytic Approach).**

Illustrations 7a–7e, which follow, are taken from pages in *United States Code Service*. The steps are indicated in the marginal notes on each reproduced page.

Illustrations 7a–7e. Steps in Using Annotated Codes (Analytic Approach).

TITLES OF UNITED STATES CODE

Step 1:
State the issue—
"Is a ship's
master liable
to persons
found in
danger at sea?"

* 1. General Provisions	26. Internal Revenue Code
2. The Congress	27. Intoxicating Liquors
* 3. The President	*28. Judiciary and Judicial Procedure
* 4. Flag and Seal, Seat of Government and the States	29. Labor
* 5. Government Organization and Employees	30. Mineral Lands and Mining
	31. Money and Finance
* 6. Surety Bonds	*32. National Guard
7. Agriculture	33. Navigation and Navigable Waters
8. Aliens and Nationality	†34. [Navy]
* 9. Arbitration	*35. Patents
*10. Armed Forces	36. Patriotic Societies and Observances
11. Bankruptcy	*37. Pay and Allowances of the Uniformed Services
12. Banks and Banking	*38. Veterans' Benefits
*13. Census	*39. Postal Service
*14. Coast Guard	40. Public Buildings, Property, and Works
15. Commerce and Trade	41. Public Contracts
16. Conservation	42. The Public Health and Welfare
*17. Copyrights	43. Public Lands
*18. Crimes and Criminal Procedure	*44. Public Printing and Documents
19. Customs Duties	45. Railroads
20. Education	46. **Shipping** [Chapters 1–17 and chapter 18 (§§ 541–590) are included in this volume]
21. Food and Drugs	
22. Foreign Relations and Intercourse	47. Telegraphs, Telephones, and Radio-telegraphs
*23. Highways	48. Territories and Insular Possessions
24. Hospitals and Asylums	49. Transportation
25. Indians	50. War and National Defense; and Appendix

Step 2:
Find the
correct title. ⟶ 46. Shipping

*This title has been enacted as law.
†This title has been superseded by the enactment of Title 10.

46 USCS §§ 1–590

Illustration 7a. Table found on inside of front cover of any volume of *United States Code Service,* Lawyers Edition. Copyright © 1979 by the Lawyers Co-Operative Publishing Company/Bancroft-Whitney Company. Reprinted with permission.

All federal laws of a general and permanent nature arranged in accordance with
the section numbering of the United
States Code and the supplements
thereto.

Step 3:
Go to the
first volume
covering the
correct title ────────────────→

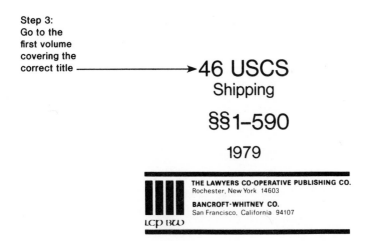

46 USCS

Shipping

§§1–590

1979

THE LAWYERS CO-OPERATIVE PUBLISHING CO.
Rochester, New York 14603

BANCROFT-WHITNEY CO.
San Francisco, California 94107

LCP BW

Illustration 7b. Title page from the first volume of Title 46 of the *United States Code Service*, Lawyers Edition. Copyright © 1979 by the Lawyers Co-Operative Publishing Company/Bancroft-Whitney Company. Reprinted with permission.

TABLE OF CONTENTS

TITLE 46 — SHIPPING

[Chapters 1–17, and Chapter 18 (§§ 541–590) are contained in this volume]

Step 4:
Go to the
analysis of
the title
and find
the correct
chapter

xi

Illustration 7c. Page xi from the first volume of Title 46 of the *United States Code Service*, Lawyers Edition. Copyright © 1979 by the Lawyers Co-Operative Publishing Company / Bancroft-Whitney Company. Reprinted with permission.

$$\boxed{\text{CHAPTER 19.   WRECKS AND SALVAGE}}$$

GENERALLY

Step 5:
Go to the
analysis of
the chapter
to find the
correct section

CROSS REFERENCES

Special navigation rules for steam vessels by Secretary of Department in which Coast Guard is operating, 33 USCS § 157.
Owners of vessels sunk in navigable channels to mark them until removed or abandoned, 33 USCS § 409.
Removal by Secretary of Army of vessels sunk in navigable waters or harbors, 33 USCS §§ 414, 415.

GENERALLY

§ 721. Vessels stranded on foreign coasts

Consuls and vice consuls, in cases where vessels of the United States are

467

Illustration 7d. First page of Chapter 19, Title 46 of the *United States Code Service,* Lawyers Edition. Copyright © 1979 by the Lawyers Co-Operative Publishing Company / Bancroft-Whitney Company. Reprinted with permission.

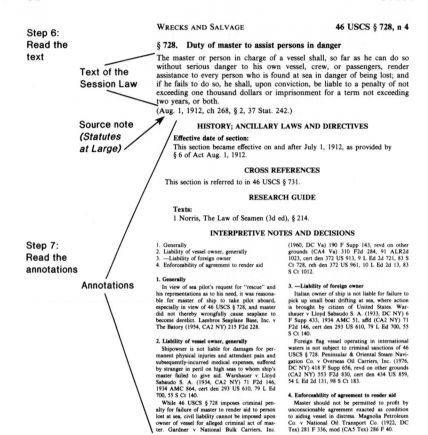

Step 6:
Read the
text

Text of the
Session Law

Source note
(Statutes
at Large)

Step 7:
Read the
annotations

Annotations

WRECKS AND SALVAGE   46 USCS § 728, n 4

§ 728.   Duty of master to assist persons in danger

The master or person in charge of a vessel shall, so far as he can do so without serious danger to his own vessel, crew, or passengers, render assistance to every person who is found at sea in danger of being lost; and if he fails to do so, he shall, upon conviction, be liable to a penalty of not exceeding one thousand dollars or imprisonment for a term not exceeding two years, or both.

(Aug. 1, 1912, ch 268, § 2, 37 Stat. 242.)

HISTORY; ANCILLARY LAWS AND DIRECTIVES

Effective date of section:

This section became effective on and after July 1, 1912, as provided by § 6 of Act Aug. 1, 1912.

CROSS REFERENCES

This section is referred to in 46 USCS § 731.

RESEARCH GUIDE

Texts:
1 Norris, The Law of Seamen (3d ed), § 214.

INTERPRETIVE NOTES AND DECISIONS

1. Generally
2. Liability of vessel owner, generally
3. —Liability of foreign owner
4. Enforceability of agreement to render aid

1. Generally

In view of sea pilot's request for "rescue" and his representations as to his need, it was reasonable for master of ship to take pilot aboard, especially in view of 46 USCS § 728, and master did not thereby wrongfully cause seaplane to become derelict. Lambros Seaplane Base, Inc. v The Batory (1954, CA2 NY) 215 F2d 228.

2. Liability of vessel owner, generally

Shipowner is not liable for damages for permanent physical injuries and attendant pain and subsequently-incurred medical expenses, suffered by stranger in peril on high seas to whom ship's master failed to give aid. Warshauer v Lloyd Sabaudo S. A. (1934, CA2 NY) 71 F2d 146, 1934 AMC 864, cert den 293 US 610, 79 L Ed 700, 55 S Ct 140.

While 46 USCS § 728 imposes criminal penalty for failure of master to render aid to person lost at sea, civil liability cannot be imposed upon owner of vessel for alleged criminal act of master. Gardner v National Bulk Carriers, Inc.

(1960, DC Va) 190 F Supp 143, revd on other grounds (CA4 Va) 310 F2d 284, 91 ALR2d 1023, cert den 372 US 913, 9 L Ed 2d 721, 83 S Ct 728, reh den 372 US 961, 10 L Ed 2d 13, 83 S Ct 1012.

3. —Liability of foreign owner

Italian owner of ship is not liable for failure to pick up small boat drifting at sea, where action is brought by citizen of United States. Warshauer v Lloyd Sabaudo S. A. (1933, DC NY) 6 F Supp 433, 1934 AMC 51, affd (CA2 NY) 71 F2d 146, cert den 293 US 610, 79 L Ed 700, 55 S Ct 140.

Foreign flag vessel operating in international waters is not subject to criminal sanctions of 46 USCS § 728. Peninsular & Oriental Steam Navigation Co. v Overseas Oil Carriers, Inc. (1976, DC NY) 418 F Supp 656, revd on other grounds (CA2 NY) 553 F2d 830, cert den 434 US 859, 54 L Ed 2d 131, 98 S Ct 183.

4. Enforceability of agreement to render aid

Master should not be permitted to profit by unconscionable agreement exacted as condition to aiding vessel in distress. Magnolia Petroleum Co. v National Oil Transport Co. (1922, DC Tex) 281 F 336, mod (CA5 Tex) 286 F 40.

473

Illustration 7e. Section 728 of Title 46 of the *United States Code Service,* Lawyers Edition. Copyright © 1979 by the Lawyers Co-Operative Publishing Company / Bancroft-Whitney Company. Reprinted with permission.

V. *Shepard's* (Statutes Edition)

A. What Does *Shepard's* Do? Annotated Codes Do the Same Thing.

When you have found a statute that is on point, the next task is to determine its current status. In other words, has the legislature added to, amended, or repealed the language of the statute in question? Have the courts interpreted it or ruled on its constitutionality?

As you have just learned, this is precisely what annotated codes do, along with their pocket parts and pamphlet supplements. Most people find annotated codes are the more convenient way of doing this. *Shepard's* can be useful, however, in certain circumstances (*e.g.* when you have superseded code citations or when you need to check a long list of citations).

Shepard's is a citation service. The statutes edition tells you if a section of the codes has been cited (mentioned) by a statute, court decision, etc. since it was first enacted.

B. Steps in "Shepardizing" a Statute

Step 1. Locate the *Shepard's* set for the jurisdiction in question.

There are *Shepard's* citators sets for every state. For the federal government use *Shepard's United States Citations.*

Step 2. Isolate the statutes parts, including supplements, from the set.

For all jurisdictions, but particularly the federal, *Shepard's* has many parts which cover not only statutes, but also court reports, administrative agency reports and regulations, special subjects (*e.g.* labor law), law review articles, and other matters. The volumes you want have a statement on the spine that reads something like: "Constitutions, Laws, Codes, Acts, Charters, Ordinances, Court Rules" or "Constitutions, Codes, Statutes."

To be positive that you have a complete set, get the latest red or uncolored supplement you can find and then check the statement on its cover that reads: "What Your Library Should Contain." *Shepard's* supplementation progresses from:

       (1) red hardbound volumes, to a

       (2) gold paperbound supplement (sometimes skipped), to a

       (3) red paperbound supplement, to an

       (4) uncolored pamphlet advance sheet.

Step 3. Locate your section of the statutes.

Start with the earliest bound volume. Look inside and you will notice that the statutory titles or codes, (or whatever are the main divisions of the state's statutes) are printed at the tops of the pages. Secondly, notice that section numbers are in bold face throughout each page. Thirdly, notice that under each section number there is a list that may include statutes, cases, attorney general opinions, and other published matters that have cited that section of the statutes. Some coded letters may also be found preceding these citations. Write down the citations that you are interested in.

Step 4. Turn to the "Abbreviations-Analysis" and "Abbreviations-Reports" tables.

These tables are found in the first few pages of *Shepard's*. They give the meanings of the coded letters and citation abbreviations.

Step 5. Check the supplements.

Repeat steps 3 and 4 through all of the supplements. (Check the "What your library should contain" statement.)

VI. Popular Name Tables

When the only statutory reference you have is the "Fungicide, Insecticide, Rodenticide Act" or the "Patman-Robinson Act" you need a popular name table. The most complete listing in one place is *Shepard's Acts and Cases by Popular Names, Federal and State.*

Popular names can also be found in annotated codes. In U.S.C.A. it is a separate table in the index volume; in U.S.C.S. it is in the "Tables" volumes. In the state codes, popular names are listed in the index as separate items, or lumped together under an entry like "popular name laws," or found as a separate table in the last index volume. The individual state *Shepard's* also have popular names tables in the statutes editions.

VII. Uniform Laws

Around the turn of the century there was considerable concern over what seemed to be an unnecessary, inconvenient, and uneconomic diversity in state laws. Two private, national organizations of outstanding lawyers, judges, and teachers came into being at that time to deal with the problem. One was the American Law Institute which concerned itself with promoting uniformity in court made law and produced the "Restatements" (see p. 145). The other organization was the National Conference of Commissioners on Uniform States Laws which did the same for legislation and produced Uniform (sometimes called Model) Acts (sometimes called Codes). The products of both groups are highly respected but are only advisory to state courts and legislatures.

The National Conference is composed of representatives from each state who are appointed by the state governors. Through a long, deliberate process of reviewing and rewriting, including multiple "tentative drafts," a uniform law is eventually produced. It is then recommended to all states for adoption. If the uniform law is introduced as a bill in a state legislature, it will go through the usual process of hearings, reports, debates, amendments, and so forth for eventual passage or nonpassage like any other state law.

The most important of all the uniform laws is the Uniform Commercial Code which has been adopted by almost all states. It can be found in a state's annotated codes like any other statute.

There are over a hundred other uniform laws. They are conveniently collected in a well annotated set called *Uniform Laws Annotated, Master Edition.* The most important annotations are the explanatory notes or comments prepared by the Commissioners themselves and the citations to court decisions. These annotations are good persuasive authority if you are researching a state law that is derived from one of the Uniform Laws.

Correct citation Forms for Uniform Laws

Unif. Juvenile Court Act §5, 9 U.L.A. 405 (1968) (Note: the date is that in which the act was last amended.)

VIII. Legislative History

A. What Is a Legislative History?

Frequently the disposition of a case is determined by a court's interpretation of some statutory language. The basic rule of statutory construction is the "plain meaning rule." That rule means that the court will carry out the assumed intent of the legislature by construing a statute according to the most common meaning ascribed to its language. Sometimes, however, the meaning may not be plain on its face, or one of the parties to an action may present extrinsic evidence of legislative intent that casts doubt on the apparent plain meaning. In such situations the court will look into the legislative history of the statute.

The term legislative history refers to those documents which are produced in the process of enacting a statute. The following is a simplified outline of this process in Congress (the interactions between the House and the Senate are ignored):[36]

(1) A bill is introduced. (BILLS are numbered and printed.)

(2) The bill is assigned to a committee. (It may die here or elsewhere along the line.)

(3) Committee hearings are held. (HEARINGS are printed under the name of the committee.)

(4) The bill is reported out of committee. (REPORTS are numbered and printed.)

(5) The bill is debated on the floor of the House and Senate. (DEBATES are dated and printed in the *Congressional Record*.)

(6) The bill, perhaps after several amendments, is passed by the Congress and signed by the President. (STATUTES are numbered and printed in the *U.S. Statutes at Large*.)

Your task in doing a legislative history is:

One: Go to a source which will give you the document citations (*i.e.* number and session of the Congress, name of committee that held the hearings, report number, and dates of the floor debate).

Two: Obtain the documents.

Three: Apply a lawyer's analytical and advocatory skills in interpreting these documents.

B. How Are Legislative Documents Used in Interpreting Statutes?

It is beyond the scope of this work to answer this question in great detail. Some of the possible uses of each of these documents, however, are briefly discussed below:

Bills: As a bill is amended during the legislative process it is reprinted. Each new printing will contain the new language. These progressive additions, deletions, and alterations in the language are direct evidence of deliberate thinking. For example, if a bill originally

---

36. This work will not deal with state legislative history. Only Congress regularly prints all of the documents used in a legislative history. Very few of the documents are available on a state level. Some research can be done, however, particularly in California and New York. Sources of help in this area include: documents librarians (at large law libraries, university libraries, state libraries, and large public libraries), legislators themselves, legislative committees, and legislative offices. Some cities have commercial services that do legislative histories for attorneys.

excluded registered pharmacists from its coverage, but such exclusionary language was dropped in the final enactment, a good argument could be made that the legislature intended to include registered pharmacists.

Hearings: These are transcripts of testimony offered by invited experts on the subject of the proposed legislation. They can be useful in indicating what information the legislature presumably had when it enacted a statute.

Reports: If a bill is not "buried" in a committee, the committee will report it out to the full legislature along with a recommendation that it pass or not pass. This is the most obviously useful of all the legislative documents in proving intent. A report will summarize the provisions of a bill and give the committee's explanation of its purpose.

Debates: The *Congressional Record* is a daily transcript of what was said on the floor of the House and Senate. Statements by legislators for or against passage of a bill can often be used to indicate how they were interpreting the meaning of its language.

C. **Law Books that Are Useful for Legislative History Research**

1. *CCH Congressional Index*

One of the most widely used indexes to the federal legislative process is published by Commerce Clearing House and is called the *CCH Congressional Index*. It is solely an index; it does not provide the documents. The steps below indicate how this tool is used, assuming you only know the subject of the bill:

Step 1. Go to the "Subject Index" to find the House or Senate bill number.

Step 2. Go to "House Bills" or "Senate Bills" to find the preamble of the bill and the name of the committee to which it was assigned.

Step 3. Go to "Status of House Bills" or "Status of Senate Bills" where you will find out what has happened to a bill if it has at least gone far enough for hearings to be held.

Step 4. Having taken steps 1, 2, and 3, you can now write down the following information:

—House or Senate bill number

—Name of the committee to which it was assigned

—House or Senate report number

—Dates of debate or other action on the House or Senate floor

Step 5. With the information gathered in step 4 you can obtain a complete legislative history from a documents librarian or other source. A complete legislative history will include the following documents:

—Printings of the various amended versions of the bill

—Transcript of committee hearings

—The committee report

—Debates from the *Congressional Record*

2. *Congressional Information Service*

The *Congressional Information Service,* in addition to being an index, provides abstracts and the full texts of some legislative history documents. It is composed of three parts: the *CIS Index,* the *CIS Annual* and the *CIS Microfiche Library.*

The *CIS Index*[37] is an excellent index to hearings, reports and other Congressional committee documents (*e.g.* "committee prints"). It has some advantages and some disadvantages as compared to the *CCH Congressional Index.* In general, it is superior in covering committee activity but inferior in covering the legislative process before a bill reaches a committee and after it leaves a committee. It does not index bills that do not reach the hearing stage nor does it provide the dates of floor debates. It also does not have current status tables of all introduced bills. These are necessary when you want to follow a bill's progress through Congress. An added feature of the *CIS Index* is that it offers abstracts of the documents it indexes. Its indexing of hearings is superior to the *CCH Congressional Index.* For example, it provides access through the names of people who have testified.

The *CIS Annual* cumulates the abstracts and indexes of the *CIS Index.*

The *CIS Microfiche Library* consists of the actual text (in microfiche) of the documents which are indexed in the *CIS Index.*

3. *U.S. Code: Congressional and Administrative News*

This service, as noted earlier, serves as the advance legislative service to West's *United States Code Annotated.* In addition, it contains some materials that are useful for an abbreviated legislative history. If you will look at this set on the shelves you will see it is divided by Congressional sessions and that within each session it is in two parts: "Laws" and "Legislative History." The "Laws" part is the advance legislative service (i.e. session laws).

---

37. The *CIS Index* is also available as a computerized, online "data base service." Some libraries subscribe to this service and access it through in-house terminals.

The "Legislative History" part prints the text of selected committee reports (sometimes in condensed form) and, occasionally, other documents. It provides citations to all of the committee reports and to the *Congressional Record*. Note that both the "Laws" and the "Legislative Histories" are arranged by public law number and have mutual references in italics after the name of the act. (See Illustrations 8a–8d.)

Correct Citation Form

BILLS: S. 2453, 91st Cong., 1st Sess. § 1 (1969)
H.R. 2077, 91st Cong., 1st Sess. § 1 (1969)

HEARINGS: *Hearings on S. 1835 Before the Subcomm. on Housing and Insurance of the Committee on Veterans' Affairs,* 93rd Cong., 1st Sess., pt. 2, at 781 (1973)

REPORTS: Senate Comm. on Governmental Affairs—Mail Order Consumer Protection Amendments of 1983, S. Rep. No. 51, 98th Cong., 1st Sess. 12

DEBATES: 115 Cong. Rec. 3177 (1969) (remarks of Senator Fulbright)

U.S. CODE: CONGRESSIONAL AND ADMINISTRATIVE NEWS: Senate Comm. on Agriculture, Nutrition and Forestry—Dairy and Tobacco Adjustment Act of 1983, S. Rep. No. 163, 98th Cong., 1st Sess. 8, *reprinted in* 1983 U.S. Code Cong. & Ad. News 1658, 1665.

Illustrations 8a–8d. A "Legislative History" from United States Code:
Congressional and Administrative News.

UNITED STATES CODE

Congressional and Administrative News

96th Congress—First Session

1979

Convened January 15, 1979

Adjourned January 3, 1980

Volume 1

This volume
contains the
"laws" section
and part of
the "legislative
history" section

PUBLIC LAWS 96–1 to 96–187
[93 Stat. pages 1 to 1369]

LEGISLATIVE HISTORY

ST. PAUL, MINN.

WEST PUBLISHING CO.

Illustration 8a. Title page from Volume 1 of the 1979 *United States Code: Congressional and Administrative News.* Copyright © 1979 by West Publishing Company. Reprinted with permission.

PUBLIC LAW 96–90 [H.R. 1301]; October 23, 1979

LOTTERIES—TRANSPORTATION OF MATERIALS
TO FOREIGN COUNTRIES

Note the reference
to the "legislative
history" section ⟶ *For Legislative History of Act, see p. 1645*

An Act to amend title 18 of the United States Code to allow the transportation
or mailing to a foreign country of material concerning a lottery authorized
by that foreign country, and for other purposes.

*Be it enacted by the Senate and House of Representatives of the
United States of America in Congress assembled,* That (a) subsection
(b) of section 1307 of title 18 of the United States Code is amended by
striking out "mailing to addresses within" and all that follows
through the end of such subsection (b) and inserting in lieu thereof
the following: "mailing—

Lottery
material,
transportation
or mailing to a
foreign country.

"(1) to addresses within a State of equipment, tickets, or
material concerning a lottery which is conducted by that State
acting under the authority of State law; or
"(2) to an addressee within a foreign country of equipment,
tickets, or material designed to be used within that foreign
country in a lottery which is authorized by the law of that foreign
country."
(b) Subsection (c) of section 1307 of title 18 of the United States Code
is amended—
(1) by inserting "(1)" after "of this section"; and
(2) by inserting "; and (2) 'foreign country' means any empire,
country, dominion, colony, or protectorate, or any subdivision
thereof (other than the United States, its territories or possessions)" before the period.
SEC. 2. Section 1953 of title 18 of the United States Code is
amended—
(1) in subsection (b), by striking out the period at the end of
such subsection and inserting in lieu thereof the following: ", or
(5) the transportation in foreign commerce to a destination in a
foreign country of equipment, tickets, or materials designed to be
used within that foreign country in a lottery which is authorized
by the laws of that foreign country."; and
(2) by adding at the end the following new subsections:

"State."

"Foreign
country."

"(d) For the purposes of this section (1) 'State' means a State of the
United States, the District of Columbia, the Commonwealth of Puerto
Rico, or any territory or possession of the United States; and (2)
'foreign country' means any empire, country, dominion, colony, or
protectorate, or any subdivision thereof (other than the United
States, its territories or possessions).

93 STAT. 698

Illustration 8b. Public Law 96–90 from the "Laws" section of Volume 1 of
the 1979 *United States Code: Congressional and Administrative News.*
Copyright © 1979 by West Publishing Company. Reprinted with
permission.

UNITED STATES CODE
Congressional and Administrative News

96th Congress—First Session

1979

———

Convened January 15, 1979
Adjourned January 3, 1980

Volume 2

This volume
contains part
of the
"legislative   LEGISLATIVE HISTORY
history" section

ST. PAUL, MINN.
WEST PUBLISHING CO.

Illustration 8c. Title page from Volume 2 of the 1979 *United States Code:*
Congressional and Administrative News. Copyright © 1979 by West
Publishing Company. Reprinted with permission.

LOTTERIES
P.L. 96–90

LOTTERIES—TRANSPORTATION OF MATERIALS
TO FOREIGN COUNTRIES

Note the
reference to
the "laws" section ————▶ *P.L. 96–90, see page 93 Stat. 698*

Report nos.,
Bill nos.,
Committee
names, dates,
and
Cong. Record
citations are
given

House Report (Judiciary Committee) No. 96–45,
Mar. 15, 1979 [To accompany H.R. 1301]

Senate Report (Judiciary Committee) No. 96–323,
Sept. 19, 1979 [To accompany S. 947]

Cong. Record Vol. 125 (1979)

DATES OF CONSIDERATION AND PASSAGE

House March 20, April 24, 1979

Senate October 10, 1979

The House bill was passed in lieu of the Senate bill.

(The House Report is set out.)

Text of House
Report is given ————▶ **HOUSE REPORT NO. 96–45**

[page 1]

The Committee on the Judiciary, to whom was referred the bill
(H.R. 1301) to amend title 18 of the United States Code to allow the
transportation or mailing to a foreign country of material concerning
a lottery authorized by that foreign country, and for other purposes,
having considered the same, report favorably thereon without amendment and recommend that the bill do pass.

PURPOSE

The bill would amend the present law to allow for the shipment
of lottery tickets and materials to a foreign country whose laws authorize a lottery.

STATEMENT

Current law allows for the transportation and shipment of lottery
tickets and other material used in connection with lotteries to States
who conduct lotteries and have enacted laws authorizing such lotteries. This bill would expand this provision to allow for the transportation or mailing of such materials to foreign countries which have
authorized lotteries by their laws.

Shipments originating in the United States to a foreign country of
material relating to a lottery conducted by that foreign country are
illegal under present law.

[page 2]

The Subcommittee on Administrative Law and Governmental Relations held a hearing on H.R. 1301. Testimony at the hearing established

2 U.S.Cong. & Adm.News '79—32   **1645**

Illustration 8d. House report on Public Law 96–90 from the "Legislative
History" section of Volume 2 of the 1979 *United States Code:
Congressional and Administrative News.* Copyright © 1979 by West
Publishing Company. Reprinted with permission.

IX. Local Codes (City and County Ordinances)

City and county ordinances follow the pattern of state and federal statutes. They are numbered in consecutive order as they are passed by the city council or county board of supervisors (or their equivalents). These separate printings of the ordinances are not generally published. When they are available it will be in codified form under major titles (zoning, public safety, sewage, etc.). Usually, the code will have a general index.

City charters are analogous to constitutions except that they are grants of power from the sovereign state rather than from the people. They are a city's "organic law."

The real problem in using local codes, ordinances, and charters is finding them. Many local governments are negligent in having them promptly published. They may not be published at all. If so, your only recourse is to go to the city hall, county office, etc. to see a copy. Sometimes a public library will be a depository.

Correct Citation Form: Municipal Codes

The Code of the City of Davis, California, § 28–1 (1980).

CHAPTER

8

Administrative Codes

I. What Are Administrative Agencies? How Do They Make Law?

Most people understand legislative law making. Judicial law making is less familiar and this concept was sketched in the first chapter. Administrative agency law making is probably least familiar and, for that reason, we shall at least note some basic ideas before getting into the sources.

The power to make law rests ultimately with us. We, the people, have adopted a constitution which sets forth, in broad terms, the machinery of government and the law making powers of each branch. The legislative branch has found that because of the great scope and complexity of its law making, it must delegate the detailed exercise of its powers to boards, commissions, bureaus, departments, etc. Congress (or a state legislature) creates administrative agencies by statutes which also define the powers and functions of each agency. Within the confines of that definition, an agency makes rules, adjudicates, issues licenses, distributes money, investigates, prosecutes, mediates, and exercises whatever other powers Congress feels is necessary for the agency to carry out a legislative purpose.

In this chapter we shall be concerned with how and where administrative agencies publish their rules and regulations. Where do you find the rules of the state Department of Alcoholic Beverage Control on getting a liquor license? Who is eligible for food stamps? Where do you find postal regulations? What rules does the state Division of Consumer Services have to control deceptive advertising? Where do you find the regulations of the N.L.R.B., the F.C.C., the F.H.A., the F.T.C., the C.A.B., the F.A.A., the S.E.C., the I.R.S., the B.I.A., etc., etc.?

II. Administrative Registers and Codes[38]

A. Federal

1. *Federal Register*

Six days a week, fifty-two weeks a year the United States Government publishes a 100 to 400 page register of its new rules and regulations, proposed rules and regulations, and notices of public meetings, requests for written comments, etc. The Federal Register Act requires that all rules, regulations, and procedures of administrative agencies that affect more than one person must be published in the *Federal Register*.[39] Like session laws, this is primary material, published in chronological order.[40]

Correct Citation Form for *Federal Register*

46 Fed. Reg. 57885 (1981) (to be codified in 7 C.F.R. Part 905)

---

38. Whenever you encounter a new area of law books, do not approach it as a mere listing of titles that you are going to have to memorize. All legal publication falls into patterns. The text of the law initially appears in chronological form and is then codified. Indexes, citators, and other search books are published. The state pattern is usually close to the federal pattern. The pattern for one kind of law is similar to another kind of law (session laws—annotated codes; reporters—digests; administrative registers—codes). The pattern is even close from country to country, at least within one legal system. You will find the counterparts of most American law books in Great Britain, Canada, Australia, and New Zealand.

39. Back in 1935 there was the case of *Panama Refining Co. v. Ryan,* 293 U.S. 388, in which the constitutionality of a regulation of the Department of the Interior was being challenged. The case went through a trial and reached the oral argument stage in the U.S. Supreme Court before someone discovered that the regulation in question had been revoked by the government before the action had ever even commenced. Neither the plaintiff oil companies, the defendant enforcement officials, nor the courts were aware of this revocation. That year, in response to this ridiculous state of affairs, Congress enacted the Federal Register Act. This act and its subsequent amendments also require publication of the *Code of Federal Regulations* (C.F.R.) and the *United States Government Manual.*

40. If you look at the *Federal Register* on the shelves you will see the daily issues that come out on newsprint. Each issue is organized in the following manner:
    —"Contents": this is a table of contents arranged alphabetically by name of agency.
    —"Rules and Regulations": they are printed department by department in no particular order. Their C.F.R. citation is given.
    —"Proposed Rules and Regulations": the purpose of this section is to give interested parties an opportunity to complain or comment.
    —"Notices": these are miscellaneous notices to the public.
    —"Reader Aids": it contains telephone numbers for assistance and a cumulative table of "C.F.R. Parts Affected."
    The "Contents" tables are cumulated monthly and then annually in separate pamphlets called *Federal Register Index.* The "C.F.R. Parts Affected" tables are also cumulated monthly and annually in separate pamphlets under the same title. The annual cumulations follow the quarterly revision schedule for C.F.R. You just have to check the dates of inclusion on all these cumulations to keep yourself oriented.

2. *Code of Federal Regulations* (C.F.R.)

All of the regulations from the *Federal Register* ARE CODIFIED IN THE *CODE OF FEDERAL REGULATIONS.*

Look at C.F.R. on the shelves and you will see that it is a set of about 150 softbound volumes in two different colors (depending on year of revision) arranged under fifty titles with an index volume at the end. The fifty titles of C.F.R. correspond to the fifty titles of U.S.C. Also on the shelves, generally after the index, should be a pamphlet titled "List of C.F.R. Sections Affected." The purpose of this list is explained under "Steps" below.

C.F.R. is kept up to date by the simple expedient of replacing individual volumes at least once a year, according to a quarterly schedule. Look on the front of any of the volumes and you will see a statement that reads: "Revised as of January 1, 19____" (or April, July, or October).

Correct Citation Form for *Code of Federal Regulations*

18 C.F.R. § 270.101 (1979)

B. State

A little over half the states publish their administrative regulations, generally in codified form. Administrative codes are available for all of the larger states. For those states that do not publish their regulations, you must contact the appropriate state agency. Typically, each agency will have a pamphlet of its regulations to distribute.[41]

III. Steps in Finding Federal Regulations

(In overview: you update C.F.R. by checking the current issues of *Federal Register.* Various cumulations of "tables of sections affected" get you from C.F.R. to *Federal Register.*) Illustrations 9a–9h show the main documents referred to in the steps below; looking in a law library is better.

Step 1. **C.F.R. Index**

Go to the C.F.R. and check under your subject in the index. It will refer you to a title and section (or part) number in the main set.

Step 2. **C.F.R. Main Set**

C.F.R. is organized by titles, parts, and sections. For example, 7

---

41. Since earliest times, governmental entities have been remiss in providing prompt and convenient publication of their laws. The only reason so much legal literature is accessible is that there has been a market for annotated codes, reporters, citators, legal encyclopedias, etc., and private publishers have stepped in. Such publishers have not felt that they could sell enough subscriptions to state administrative codes in many states to cover the high costs of printing, compiling, editing, indexing, and supplementing.

C.F.R. §55.160 means title 7, part 55, section 160.[42] After reading the text of the regulation, note the revision date on the front cover. You now have to see if the *Federal Register* has published any changes in your regulation since that date.

Step 3. **Sections Affected—Basic Cumulation**

Find the latest "List of C.F.R. Sections Affected" (generally on the shelf after the index). Check under your reference. The "List" will refer you to a page in the *Federal Register*. Check the dates of coverage on the front cover of the list.

Step 4. **Sections Affected—Monthly Cumulation**

Go to the *Federal Register*. In the back of the last issue of each month there is a "C.F.R. Parts Affected" list for that month. This monthly cumulation may also be available as a separate pamphlet. Check for each month after the basic cumulation (Step 3).

Step 5. **Sections Affected—Latest Cumulation for Current Month**

In the back of each daily issue of the *Federal Register* there is a "C.F.R. Parts Affected During . . ." list. Check the latest issue.

Step 6. *Federal Register—Text*

Take the references from the sections affected lists and go to the *Federal Register* for the text of any changes to what you originally read in C.F.R. The pages in the *Federal Register* are numbered consecutively for an entire year, starting with the first issue in January.

IV. Finding the Regulation When You Have the Statute and Vice Versa

As explained earlier, administrative agencies have no inherent constitutional law making authority. Their authority is derived from the legislature. All administrative regulations have a particular authorizing statute ("enabling act") or executive document[43] behind them.

There is seldom any problem in finding the regulation when you have the statute or the other way around. Both the *United States Code Annotated* (U.S.C.A.) and the *United States Code Service* (U.S.C.S.) provide references to C.F.R. as part of their annotations under each section. C.F.R., in turn, provides references to the U.S.C. or other authority as a note at the beginning of a group of regulations. The index volume of C.F.R. has parallel tables that will take you from the statute, executive order, etc. to the regulation.

42. For most purposes lawyers do not take note of such subdivisions as "parts," "chapters," "subchapters," etc.—simply knowing the title and section will get you there. The same is true of annotated codes. Refer only to the main division and the section number, *e.g.* Title 7, §55.160 or Penal Code §122a.

43. Executive documents are the various forms of law making texts issuing from the chief executive. On the federal level they include proclamations, executive orders, and reorganization plans. Some administrative agencies have been created by executive orders which were authorized by statute. Executive documents are published in a series called *Weekly Compilation of Presidential Documents,* as required under the Federal Register Act.

Illustrations 9a–9h. Basic Steps in Using an Administrative Code—*Code of Federal Regulations* and *Federal Register.*

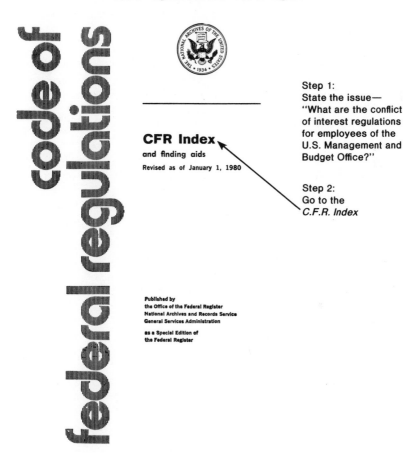

Step 1:
State the issue—
"What are the conflict of interest regulations for employees of the U.S. Management and Budget Office?"

Step 2:
Go to the
C.F.R. Index

Illustration 9a. Title page from *C.F.R. Index.*

employees of Commission, 17 CFR 140

Exchange disciplinary or other adverse action review, 17 CFR 9

Community Services Administration

Contracts and grants, reporting and review procedures, 45 CFR 1026

Employees standards of conduct, 45 CFR 1015

Consumer Product Safety Commission

Employee membership and participation in voluntary standards, 16 CFR 1031

Employee standards of conduct, 16 CFR 1030

Cost Accounting Standards Board, 4 CFR 302

Defense Department

Participation of personnel in activities of private associations, 32 CFR 91

Standards of conduct, 32 CFR 40

Defense Logistics Agency, 32 CFR 1289

Energy Department, 10 CFR 1010

Environmental Protection Agency

Employee responsibilities and conduct, 40 CFR 3

Government procurement, 41 CFR 15-1

Grants, procurement and procurement systems of grantees, subagreements, 40 CFR 33

Equal Employment Opportunity Commission, 29 CFR 1600

Executive Office of the President, 3 CFR 100

Export-Import Bank, 12 CFR 400

Farm Credit Administration, 12 CFR 601

Federal Communications Commission, 47 CFR 19

Federal Deposit Insurance Corporation, 12 CFR 336

Federal Emergency Management Agency, 44 CFR 3

Federal Energy Regulatory Commission, 18 CFR 3c

Federal Home Loan Bank Board, 12 CFR 511

Federal Labor Relations Authority and Federal Service Impasses Panel, 5 CFR 2415

Federal Maritime Commission, 46 CFR 500

Federal Mediation and Conciliation Service, 29 CFR 1400

Federal Mine Safety and Health Review Commission, 29 CFR 2703

Federal Reserve System, 12 CFR 264

Federal Trade Commission, 16 CFR 5

Food and Drug Administration, 21 CFR 19

45 CFR 73a

Foreign Claims Settlement Commission, 45 CFR 502

General Accounting Office, 4 CFR 6

General Services Administration

Foreign gifts and decorations, utilization, donation, and disposal, 41 CFR 101-49

Standards of conduct, 41 CFR 105-735

Health, Education, and Welfare Department, 45 CFR 73

Housing and Urban Development Department, 24 CFR 0

Indian Claims Commission, 25 CFR 500

Inter-American Foundation, 22 CFR 1001

Intergovernmental Relations Advisory Commission, 5 CFR 1700

Interior Department, 43 CFR 20

International Boundary and Water Commission, U.S. and Mexico, 22 CFR 1100

International Communication Agency, 22 CFR 500

International Trade Commission, 19 CFR 200

Interstate Commerce Commission, 49 CFR 1000

Justice Department, 28 CFR 45

Labor Department, 29 CFR 0

Management and Budget Office, 5 CFR 1300

Step 3: Check the Index under topic and subtopic

103

Illustration 9b. Page from *C.F.R. Index.*

code of federal regulations

5

Administrative Personnel

Revised as of January 1, 1980

CONTAINING
A CODIFICATION OF DOCUMENTS
OF GENERAL APPLICABILITY
AND FUTURE EFFECT

AS OF JANUARY 1, 1980

With Ancillaries

Published by
the Office of the Federal Register
National Archives and Records Service
General Services Administration

as a Special Edition of
the Federal Register

Step 4:
Go to the correct title

(Note the date of this volume. See illus. 9e.)

Illustration 9c. Title page from Title 5 of *C.F.R.*

§ 1300.735–1

SUBCHAPTER A—ADMINISTRATIVE PROCEDURES

PART 1300—STANDARDS OF CONDUCT

AUTHORITY: E.O. 11222, 30 FR 6469, May 8, 1965, 3 CFR, 1965 Comp., P. 306; 5 CFR 735.104.

SOURCE: 41 FR 24682, June 17, 1976, unless otherwise noted.

§ 1300.735–1 **Purpose.**

(a) The maintenance of unusually high standards of honesty, integrity, impartiality, and conduct by regular employees and special Government employees is essential to assure the proper performance of Government business and the maintenance of confidence by citizens in their Government. The avoidance of misconduct and conflicts of interest on the part of regular employees and special Government employees through informed judgment is indispensable to the maintenance of these standards.

(b) This part is intended to foster the foregoing concepts. It is issued in compliance with the requirements of Executive Order No. 11222 of May 8, 1965, and is based upon the provisions of that order, the regulations of the Civil Service Commission issued thereunder (Part 735 of this title), and the statutes cited elsewhere in this part.

§ 1300.735–2 **Definitions.**

(a) For the purposes of this part, the terms "employee," "regular employee," and "regular Government employee" mean any officer or employee of the Office of Management and Budget except a special Government employee.

(b) The term "special Government employee" means an officer or employee who is retained, designated, appointed, or employed by the Office of Management and Budget to perform with or without compensation, for not more than 130 days during any period of 365 consecutive days temporary duties either on a full-time or intermittent basis.

(c) The term "person" means an individual, a corporation, a company, an association, a firm, a partnership, a society, a joint stock company, or any other organization or institution.

§ 1300.735–3 **Special Government employees.**

Except where specifically provided otherwise, or where limited in terms or by the context to regular employees or regular Government employees, all provisions of this part relating to em-

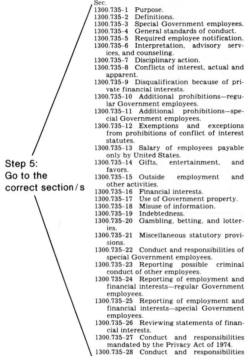

Step 5:
Go to the
correct section/s

Illustration 9d. Page from Title 5 of *C.F.R.*

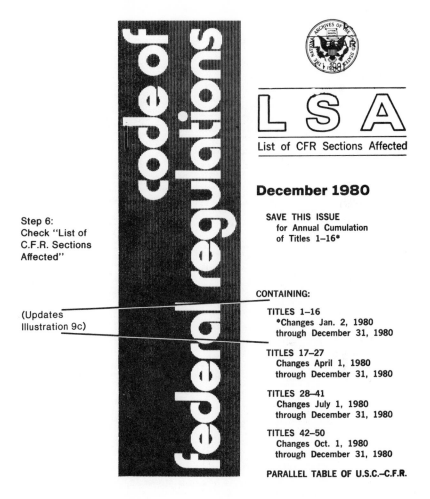

Step 6:
Check "List of
C.F.R. Sections
Affected"

(Updates
Illustration 9c)

LSA

List of CFR Sections Affected

December 1980

SAVE THIS ISSUE
for Annual Cumulation
of Titles 1–16*

CONTAINING:

TITLES 1–16
*Changes Jan. 2, 1980
through December 31, 1980

TITLES 17–27
Changes April 1, 1980
through December 31, 1980

TITLES 28–41
Changes July 1, 1980
through December 31, 1980

TITLES 42–50
Changes Oct. 1, 1980
through December 31, 1980

PARALLEL TABLE OF U.S.C.–C.F.R.

Illustration 9e. Title page from "List of C.F.R. Sections Affected."

14   LSA—LIST OF CFR SECTIONS AFFECTED

CHANGES JANUARY 2 THROUGH DECEMBER 31, 1980

Step 7:
Look for
references
to your title
and section/s

Title 5, Chapter I—Continued

	Page
(a), (b), and (f)(1) republished	85687
870.601—870.602 (Subpart F) Revised; interim	80475
870.601 (b) revised; interim	84958
(b) republished	85688
870.701—870.702 (Subpart G) Revised; interim	80476
871 Heading revised; interim; eff. 4–1–81	84958
Heading republished	85688
871.101 Revised; interim; eff. 4–1–81	84958
Republished	85688
871.202 Revised; interim; eff. 3–1–81	84958
Republished	85688
871.204 (b) revised; (d) added; interim; eff. 3–1–81	84958
(b) and (d) republished	85688
871.205 (e) added; interim; eff. 3–1–81	84959
(e) republished	85688
871.206 Revised	23636
871.207 Removed	23636
871.401 (c) revised; (g) added; interim; eff. 4–1–81	84959
(c) and (g) republished	85689
871.501 (b) revised; (c) and (d) redesignated as (d) and (e); new (c) added; interim	84959
(b) and (c) republished	85689
871.601 Revised; interim	84959
Republished	85689
871.604 (b) revised; interim	84959
(b) republished	85689
872 Added; interim	84958
Republished	85689
873 Added; interim	84963
Republished	85692
890.103 Revised; final	23637
890.104 Revised	23637
890.105 Removed; new 890.105 redesignated from 890.106	23637
890.106 Redesignated as 890.105; new 890.106 redesignated from 189.107	23637
890.107 Redesignated as 890.106; new 890.107 redesignated from 189.108	23637
890.108 Redesignated as 890.107	23637
890.201 (a)(10) added; interim	85696
890.302 (b), (c), (d), and (e) redesignated as (d), (e), (f), and (g); new (b) and (c) added; interim eff. 1–2–81	76088

	Page
890.701—890.702 (Subpart G) Added; interim	12376
Added; final	48099
890.701 Amended	81728
891.105 Revised; final	23637
891.106 Revised	23637
891.107 Removed	23637
891.401 Revised	30611
900.204 (h)(2) and (3) nomenclature change correction	3565
900.701—900.710 (Subpart G) Added	75569
930.207 Revised; eff. 1–8–81	81030
1001.735–401 Introductory text revised	83473
1001.735–409 (a) revised	83473

Chapter II—Merit Systems Protection Board

	Page
1201 Appendix II amended	6537, 34861
1251 Authority citation correctly added	2837
1252 Authority citation correctly added	2837
1253 Authority citation correctly added	2837
1254 Authority citation correctly added	2837
1255 Authority citation correctly added	2837
1260 Authority citation correctly added	2837
1261 Authority citation corrected	2837, 10305

Chapter III—Office of Management and Budget

	Page
1304 Added	84007

Chapter XIV—Federal Labor Relations Authority, General Counsel of the Federal Labor Relations Authority and Federal Service Impasses Panel

	Page
Chapter XIV Revised	3486
Appendix A amended	80467
2400 (Subchapter A and Part) Revised	3487
2411—2415 (Subchapter B) Revised	3488
2411 Revised	3488
2412 Revised	3491
2413 Revised	3494
2414 Revised	3495

This number refers to
a page in the 1980
Federal Register

Illustration 9f. Page from "List of C.F.R. Sections Affected."

12-22-80
Vol. 45—No. 247
BOOK 1:
Pages
84005–84400

BOOK 2:
Pages
84401–84760

Step 8:
Go to the
correct issue
of the
Federal Register

federal register

Book 1 of 2 Books
Monday, December 22, 1980

Pages included in this issue.
(Pages are numbered
consecutively throughout
the year.)

Highlights

84005 **Civil service status of CETA participants**
Executive order implementing noncompetitive
conversion procedures Executive order

84380 **Airports** DOT/FAA proposes changes to rule
which establishes the number of takeoffs or
landings at high density airports; comments by
1–2–81 (Part III of this issue)

84390 **Mineral Resources** Interior/BLM and NPS
propose joint rule regarding the leasing of minerals;
comments by 1–21–81 (Part V of this issue)

84384 **Asbestos** CPSC requests manufacturers and
importers of specified categories of consumer
products to furnish information concerning the use
of asbestos; comments by 2–20–81 (Part IV of this
issue)

84046 **Housing** HUD/FHC requires the Secretary to offer
to amend each rent supplement contract, prior to
10–8–84; effective 3–2–81

84048 **Housing** HUD/NVACP defines the term "referral"
as used in reference to Anti-Kickback provisions of
the Real Estate Settlement Procedure Act; effective
3–2–81; comments by 2–20–81

CONTINUED INSIDE

Illustration 9g. Title page from *Federal Register* of December 22, 1980.

(Note statutory authority for
the new regulation.)

84007

Rules and Regulations

Federal Register

Vol. 45, No. 247

Monday, December 22, 1980

This section of the FEDERAL REGISTER contains regulatory documents having general applicability and legal effect, most of which are keyed to and codified in the Code of Federal Regulations, which is published under 50 titles pursuant to 44 U.S.C. 1510.
The Code of Federal Regulations is sold by the Superintendent of Documents. Prices of new books are listed in the first FEDERAL REGISTER issue of each month.

OFFICE OF MANAGEMENT AND BUDGET

5 CFR Part 1304

[OMB Manual—Section 460]

Post Employment Conflict of Interest

AGENCY: Office of Management and Budget.

ACTION: Final Rule.

**Step 9:
Read
the
changes**

SUMMARY: This section sets forth OMB's policy and procedures which implement the Ethics in Government Act of 1978 and the Office of Personnel Management's regulations for determining violations of restrictions on post-employment activities and for exercising OMB's administrative enforcement authority. These regulations bar certain acts by former Government employees which may give the appearance of making unfair use of prior Government employment and affiliations.

EFFECTIVE DATE: June 1, 1980.

FOR FURTHER INFORMATION CONTACT: Mrs. Lee Dowd, Office of General Counsel (202) 395–5600.

SUPPLEMENTARY INFORMATION: This part is not published for public comment because it relates to agency management and personnel matters.
For the reasons set forth in the preamble, Part 1304, entitled Post Employment Conflict of Interest is added to Subchapter A, Chapter III of Title 5 of the CFR to read as follows:

PART 1304—POST EMPLOYMENT CONFLICT OF INTEREST

Sec.
1304.4601 Purpose.
1304.4604 Definitions.
1304.4605 Post-Employment Restrictions.
1304.4606 Exemptions.
1304.4607 Advice to Former Government Employees.

Sec.
1304.4608 Administrative Enforcement Procedures.

Authority: Title V, Section 501(a), Pub. L. 95–521, as amended, 92 Stat. 1864; and Sections 1 and 2, Pub. L. 96–28, 93 Stat. 76 [18 U.S.C. 207]; 5 CFR 737.

§ 1304.4601 Purpose.

(a) This section sets forth OMB's policy and procedures under the Ethics in Government Act of 1978, 18 U.S.C. 207, and the Office of Personnel Management's implementing regulations, 5 CFR Part 737, for determining violations of restrictions on post-employment activities and for exercising OMB's administrative enforcement authority.

(b) These regulations bar certain acts by former Government employees which may reasonably give the appearance of making unfair use of prior Government employment and affiliations. OMB acts on the premise that it has the primary responsibility for the enforcement of restrictions on post-employment activities and that criminal enforcement by the Department of Justice should be undertaken only in cases involving aggravated circumstances.

(c) These regulations do not incorporate possible additional restrictions contained in a professional code of conduct to which an employee may also be subject.

(d) Any person who holds a Government position after June 30, 1979, is subject to the restrictions under this section; except that the new provisions applicable to Senior employees designated by the Director of the Office of Government Ethics are effective February 28, 1980.

§ 1304.4604 Definitions.

(a) "Government Employee" includes any officer or employee of the Executive Branch, those appointed or detailed under 5 U.S.C. 3374, and Special Government Employees. It does not include an individual performing services for the United States as an independent contractor under a personal service contract.

(b) "Former Government Employee" means one who was, and no longer is, a Government employee.

(c) "Special Government Employee" means an officer or employee of an agency who is retained, designated, appointed, or employed to perform temporary duties on a full-time or intermittent basis for not more than 130

days during any period of 365 consecutive days. This applies whether the Special Government Employee is compensated or not.

(d) "Senior Employee" means an employee or officer as designated in the statute or by the Director of the Office of Government Ethics. The Director of the Office of Government Ethics has designated civilians who have significant decision-making or supervisory responsibility and are paid at or equivalent to GS–17 or above as Senior Employees. Civilians paid at the Executive level are automatically designated by statute as Senior Employees. (A list of Senior Employee positions is found at 5 CFR 737.33.)

§ 1304.4605 Post-Employment Restrictions.

(a) General Restrictions Applicable to All Former Government Employees:

(1) *Permanent Bar.* A former Government employee is restricted from acting as a representative before an agency as to a particular matter involving a specific party if the employee participated personally and substantially in that matter as a Government employee. The government employee is also restricted from making any oral or written communication to an agency with the intent to influence on behalf of another person as to a particular matter involving a specific party if the former Government employee participated personally and substantially in that matter as a Government employee.

(2) *Two-Year Bar.* (i) A former Government employee is restricted for two years from acting as a representative before an agency as to a particular matter involving a specific party if the employee had official responsibility for that matter. The former Government employee is also restricted for two years from making any oral or written communication to any agency with the intent to influence on behalf of another person as to a particular matter involving a specific party if the employee had official responsibility for that matter.

(ii) In order to be a matter for which the former Government employee had official responsibility, the matter must actually have been pending under the employee's responsibility within the period of one year prior to the termination of such responsibility.

Illustration 9h. Page 84007 from *Federal Register* of December 22, 1980.

V. "Shepardizing" C.F.R.

Shepard's Code of Federal Regulations Citations is a new service. This citator takes you from C.F.R. (or an executive document) to any cases that have cited it. Its coverage, at present, only goes back to the 1977–1978 period.

VI. Government Manuals

One of the difficulties of researching administrative law is the complexity of the organizational structure of administrative agencies. We often do not know what agencies exist and what their functions are. It is frequently not enough to get the text of the regulations. What to a mere citizen seems to be a single activity, the government will view as multifaceted and will regulate it with a number of agencies. For example, you cannot understand the federal government's ambivalent attitude toward recreational use of public land unless you know that the National Park Service is under the Interior Department and the National Forest Service is under the Agricultural Department, and that these two departments have differing and sometimes conflicting roles.

These government manuals will generally list for each agency: the staff, addresses, functions, organizational structure, and statutory authority. They are indexed. *The United States Government Manual* comes out yearly. In it you will find such favorites as The Center for Short-lived Phenomena and the American Battle Monuments Commission.

The state manuals go under various names, including register, blue book, directory, guide, yearbook, almanac, and handbook. They are generally not published annually; sometimes they are only issued at the beginning of a gubernatorial administration.[44]

---

44. If your state government issues a state "roster" or a telephone directory, it will be the best current source for names, addresses, phone numbers, and even organizational structure.

9

Court Rules

I. What Are "Court Rules"?

Inexperienced researchers are often confused about the sources for court rules because of the ambiguity of the expression itself. In its broad sense it means all laws, from any source, pertaining to court structure, personnel, administration, and procedure. In its narrow sense it means those rules adopted by the courts themselves to govern their procedures. Using the broad definition, court rules come from three sources: constitutions, legislatures, and courts. The latter can also be subdivided onto two levels: whole judicial systems and individual courts.

II. Sources of Court Rules

A. Constitutions

Typically, a state constitution will declare the organizational structure of the judiciary: what courts there will be, their jurisdiction, and how they will be administered. It may set forth the number of judges in each court, their term of office, their qualifications, how they will be selected and removed, restrictions on their outside activities, and some basic rules on salaries. It may also establish commissions on judicial tenure, appointments, or qualifications. Finally, in some states, it may set down some fairly detailed rules on court procedure, particularly appellate procedure.

B. Legislature versus the Courts

The jurisdiction of the legislature versus that of the courts in making court rules is disputed. What is evolving over the years, however, is a generally recognized distinction between a legislative realm within which rights and duties (public policy) are created, and a judicial realm within which courts provide for their efficient functioning.[45]

1. Legislature

You will find the legislative court rules in the state or federal annotated codes under such headings as civil procedure, criminal procedure, evidence, courts, practice, judiciary, and such special practice areas as probate, family practice, and juvenile practice.

2. Courts

When experienced lawyers refer to "court rules" they generally mean the rules that the courts have adopted themselves. These court rules come from two levels.

a. Rules for an Entire Judicial System

Typically, the highest court in a system has the authority to prescribe a uniform code of rules that applies to all of the courts within the system. Sometimes the supreme court is aided in this task by a judicial council, conference committee, or similar body.

These court rules are generally included as an added feature in the state's statutory code in a volume/s (often paperbound) entitled "Rules Volume," "Rules of Court," "Civil Rules and Criminal Rules," etc. They will generally be subdivided according to the hierarchy of the system. For example: appellate rules, general trial court rules, municipal court rules, and justice court rules.[46]

b. Rules for Individual Courts

All courts have the inherent power to adopt rules that aid in the efficient carrying out of their business. Individual courts have their own rules which must be consistent, of course, with the systemwide court rules. They usually cover such details as court calendars, filing fees, deadlines, and how and what documents must be submitted for particular purposes.

---

45. On top of this theoretical distinction, however, is the fact that the mere introduction of judicial councils and the increase in judicial administrative staffs have allowed the courts to extend their rule making realm at the expense of busy legislatures.
46. Another handy source for these systemwide rules will be the state pleading and practice books. Also, as court systems adopt rules, or amendments or additions thereto, they will publish such in their reporters. The latter are not a very convenient source of rules, however, since they are neither promptly published nor in codified form.

Copies of these local rules are available from the clerk's office of the court in question. In some of the larger states, local legal publishers (especially legal newspaper publishers) publish these rules. Sometimes state pleading and practice sets contain the rules of at least the major trial courts in that state.

III. Publication of Federal Court Rules

The various federal court rules may be found in a variety of practitioners manuals, rules services, form books, separate pamphlets, and reporters. Probably the two most accessible sources, however, are the annotated codes and the major pleading and practice sets.

A. Annotated Codes

Both U.S.C.A. and U.S.C.S. have special volumes containing the federal court rules, including the Federal Rules of Civil Procedure, Criminal Procedure, Appellate Procedure, and Evidence; plus the Rules of the Supreme Court, the individual circuits of the Court of Appeals, and the various special courts (Claims, Customs, etc.). They do not contain the rules for the individual district courts. In U.S.C.A. these special volumes are found accompanying Title 28 "Judiciary and Judicial Procedure" and Title 18 "Crimes and Procedure." In U.S.C.S. they are in "Court Rules" volumes toward the end of the set.

B. Pleading and Practice Sets

The major sets contain most of the federal court rules. They include: West Publishing Co.'s *Federal Practice and Procedure,* Lawyers Cooperative Publishing Co.'s *Federal Procedure,* Matthew Bender Publishing Co.'s *Moore's Federal Practice,* and Callaghan Publishing Co.'s *Cyclopedia of Federal Procedure.* Callaghan also publishes *Federal Local Court Rules* which contains the various district court rules relating to civil procedure and the rules of the various circuits of the courts of appeals.

Correct Citation Form: Court Rules

Tenn. R. Civ. P. 15.01 (1981)
Fed. R. Evid. 602 (1975)

10

Treaties[47]

I. The Importance of Treaty Law for the Average Lawyer

Article 6, clause 2 of the United States Constitution provides that treaties, along with the Constitution and the enactments of Congress, are "the supreme law of the land." There is a tendency to regard treaty research as the special concern of international lawyers, but there are a number of everyday occurrences which are governed by provisions of treaties to which the United States is a party. For example, when an American citizen earns income in a foreign country he has a potential problem of double taxation which may be provided for in a bilateral treaty. Another common situation covered by treaties is the distribution of property located in another country but owned by an American decedent. Treaties, of course, are of central importance in the entire area of international business transactions, including such matters as tariffs, copyright, patent, and trademark. Finally, conservation and exploitation of natural resources (oceans, rivers, wildlife, etc.) are often covered by treaties.[48]

---

47. This work only covers researching those treaties to which the United States is a party.
48. Treaty law is part of a somewhat amorphous and often misunderstood branch of law called "International Law." A few basic definitions and facts can be helpful in orienting a novice.

   There is Public International Law and a Private International Law. Public International Law is that body of laws and usage governing relations between nations (or other international bodies). A more descriptive name is Law of Nations. The Law of Nations works because countries generally find it in their best long term interests to acquiesce. Of course, there is no super government, including the United Nations, with significant sanctioning power. The sources for this branch of the law are: treaties; customs and practices of such long standing that they have become recognized as rules; the writings of authoritative scholars; and court and arbitration decisions, both national and international.

   Court and arbitration decisions come from a number of sources. There is an International Court of Justice which sits at The Hague, a city in the Netherlands. It can only decide controversies which have been willingly submitted to it by both parties. Although national court decisions are only binding within a court's national boundaries, they are cited in international disputes as persuasive authority. There are a number

II. Publications Used in Treaty Research

A. The Text of the United States Treaties

1. *Statutes at Large* (Stat.)

Until 1950, the United States published the text of its treaties in *Statutes at Large,* along with the session laws.

2. *United States Treaties and Other International Agreements* (U.S.T.)

In 1950, the federal government stopped publishing its treaties in *Statutes at Large* and introduced U.S.T. About three or four bound volumes come out each year. Prior to being bound, the treaties and other international agreements appear in individual pamphlet form (similar to the federal "slip laws" and "slip opinions"). Each document is given a consecutive T.I.A.S. number (Treaties and other International Act Series).

B. Indexes to United States Treaties

1. Current Index—*Treaties in Force*

As its title indicates, this annual index covers United States treaties that are currently in force. It is in two parts. Part 1 covers bilateral treaties which are listed first by country and then by subject within each country. Part 2 covers multilateral treaties, which are listed by subject.

2. Historical Indexes

a. *United States Treaties and Other International Agreements Cumulative Index 1776–1949.* Compiled by Kavass and Michael.

This index includes all treaties and other agreements the United States entered into from its founding to the time it stopped publishing them in *Statutes at Large.* The four volumes respectively list agreements by number, date, country, and subject.

---

of arbitration institutions in cities throughout the world which operate under various published sets of rules. International contracts will frequently provide that disputes will be resolved by certain arbitration institutes, applying specified rules.

Private International Law operates only within one jurisdiction. It is that body of legal rules that a court applies when the controversy involves a foreign element, *i.e.* foreign facts or persons. In the United States, we call this branch of the law Conflict of Laws.

In practical terms, most lawyers in the international arena practice what is called Multinational Law. In other words they are facilitating activities, largely commercial, that involve the law of more than one country.

b. **U.S.T. Cumulative Index 1950–1970.** Compiled by Kavass and Sprudzs.

This picks up where the prior index leaves off, starting with the initiation of the U.S.T. series. It has the same four volume arrangement.

C. "Shepardizing" Treaties

The "Statutes" editions of *Shepard's United States Citations* and the state citators have citations to cases, treaties, and other documents affecting treaties. Look under the Stats. or U.S.T. citation, as appropriate.

D. Information on Pending Treaties

Finding the status or text of treaties that are "in process" is a task for a specialist, like a documents librarian.[49]

Correct Citation Form: Treaties

Bilateral:

Treaty of Commerce and Navigation, July 2, 1862, United States-Ottoman Empire, 12 Stat. 1213, T.S. No. 156.

Multilateral;

International Energy Agency, Long-Term Co-Operation Programme, March 23, 1976, 27 U.S.T. 233, T.I.A.S. 8229.

49. Typically, U.S. treaties go through the following stages:
   —*signing* by the representatives of the countries involved
   —*approval* by a 2/3 vote of the Senate
   —*ratification* by the President
   —*exchange of ratifications* by the countries
   —*proclamation* by the President
The effective date of a treaty is the date of ratification, unless the terms of the treaty specify otherwise. There can be a long delay between the critical stages of signing and Senate approval. (The U.S. representatives signed the Genocide Treaty in 1948; it is still in the Senate Foreign Relations Committee.) Because of this delay, it is important to be able to find the text and information on treaties before they appear in the T.I.A.S. series. The following three titles are the most important to know.
   (1) *Senate Executive Documents*
        It is surprisingly difficult to obtain the text of treaties during the period between signing and Senate approval. The text, of course, is available to the U.S. Senate and is published in a series called *Senate Executive Documents*. These documents are initially confidential, however, and are not available until released for publication by the Senate.
   (2) *Department of State Bulletin*
        This publication is "The Official Monthly Record of United States Foreign Policy." It contains summaries of some U.S. treaties, a monthly "Current Actions" listing of treaties, and a listing of Department Press Releases. Press releases sometimes contain the text of treaties after signing.
   (3) *C.C.H. Congressional Index*
        In addition to its legislative history coverage (see p. 97), the *Congressional Index* contains a table for treaties that indicates their current status in the Senate approval process. The table is found under the tab labeled "Reorganization Plans-Treaties-Nominations."

SECTION

Commentaries

Section Outline

Chapter 16: Form Books
  I.   How They Are Used
  II. Types of Form Books
        A. Business Form Books
        B. Procedural Form Books
        C. Statutory Form Books
        D. Special Form Books
        E. Practitioners' Manuals

Chapter 17: Legal Directories
  I.   *Martindale-Hubbell*
  II. Other Legal Directories

Chapter 18: Dictionaries and *Words and Phrases*

Preface

Legal commentaries include those works in which experts summarize, explain, criticize, or otherwise comment on legal topics. Such writings are almost always extensively annotated to cases and codes.

Research, using only cases and codes, includes:

(1) Finding the law (statutes, cases, regulations, etc.).
(2) Interpreting the law (*i.e.* holdings, statutory interpretation, etc.)
(3) Synthesizing the law (*e.g.* what rule of law can we extrapolate from a line of cases?).
(4) Constructing arguments and counter arguments.

This kind of research is intellectually satisfying and calls for the use of a lawyer's fundamental skills. But it is expensive. It is not suggested that you will never need to do original research; but, unless you are entering an academic discipline, TIME will always be a *major* constraint on your research. You must learn to research competently, but expeditiously. This requires a knowledge of the sources of legal commentary. If you can find a law review article, or a chapter in a text book, or a section in a looseleaf service, or an *A.L.R.* annotation on point—you may find that the author has done much of the work for you.

11

Periodicals (Law Reviews)

I. A Unique Source

There are nearly 350 periodicals dealing with American law. The law reviews and other special subject journals published by the law schools account for most of them. The rest are published by professional societies, research foundations, and bar associations.

Why do we have law reviews? Of course, "publish or perish" in the law schools stimulates a lot of this writing, but the other reason is the need for literature on topics which are *very current* or *very specific.*

Many legal subjects are so new that there is little law on the topic. It takes a long time for a body of case law to develop. Bills can be re-introduced in legislatures for years before they are ever enacted. Law review writing, therefore, fills a gap by being an excellent medium for scholarly writing on developing areas of the law.

Law Reviews are also a rich source of information on countless narrow topics. It is a revelation for the beginner to stroll through the legal periodicals section of a good sized law library. When you look at those thousands of volumes, with their tens of thousands of articles, you cannot help but feel that the chances are excellent of finding an article on any subject you want.

Correct Citation Form

Ayer, *Water Quality Control at Lake Tahoe,* 58 Calif. L. Rev. 1273, 1281 (1970)

II. Legal Periodical Indexes

A. *Index to Legal Periodicals*[50]

If you have used *Reader's Guide to Periodical Literature,* you will have no problems with the *Index to Legal Periodicals* which is published by the same company and has much the same organization.

It is often best to start your search with the list of subject headings which appears at the beginning of any of the volumes. It is easier to narrow in on your subject headings while scanning this list than by flipping back and forth in the main part of the volume. You are also less likely to overlook promising headings.

The *Index to Legal Periodicals* is presently divided into the following parts:

—"Subject and Author Index"[51]
—"Table of Cases Commented Upon"
—"Book Review Index"

The latter two parts are self explanatory. The "Subject and Author Index" interfiles subject and author entries in the same alphabet. Full entries are only given under the subject. Looking under author, you get a reference like: "Corporations (F)," which means you must look under the subject "Corporations" and then for the title of an article that starts with the letter "F."

B. *Current Law Index*

This is an important new service that indexes legal periodical articles published since January 1980. It is computer produced with full listings under both subject and author/title plus a table of cases and a table of statutes. Monthly issues are published with quarterly and annual cumulations. It indexes a greater number of periodicals than the *Index to Legal Periodicals* which only covers periodicals that "regularly publish legal articles of high quality and permanent reference value."

---

50. The present *Index to Legal Periodicals* started its coverage in 1926. A prior series, with some overlap, is generally known as the "Jones-Chipman Index." Its coverage extends back through the 19th Century.
51. Until the 13th cumulation in 1964, subjects and authors were listed separately.

C. *Legal Resources Index*

This is another new service from the same company that publishes *Current Law Index.*[52] It is a "COM" publication (computer-output-microform) and is read on a special high speed microfilm reader/printer. Its coverage includes what is in the *Current Law Index* plus articles from major legal newspapers, articles on law from general periodicals and newspapers, and some matters from legal monographs and government publications. A convenient feature is that each monthly issue cumulates all prior issues; there are no supplements to check. Its coverage began with January 1980.

III. *Shepard's Law Review Citations*

This is the source to go to if you have a law review article and want to find if it has been cited by the courts or by other law reviews. Its coverage began with 1957 citations.

---

52. The company's name is Information Access Corporation. An "on-line" version of the *Legal Resource Index* started in July 1980.

12

Hornbooks, Manuals, Treatises and Looseleaf Services

I. Hornbooks

You may be already familiar with these one volume student texts. They provide a summary treatment of standard law school subjects. Examples include *Prosser on Torts, McCormick on Evidence,* and the titles in West's "Nutshell Series."

II. Practitioners' Manuals

These are designed for the practicing lawyer. They tend somewhat toward a how-to-do-it style and frequently contain forms, "practice tips," checklists, and other practical aids. Absolute beginners who turn to these manuals, however, are generally disillusioned to find that very few of these *really* tell you how to do it.[53] The majority of these books are composed like most legal writing: the cases, statutes, and other laws are collected, organized, synthesized, and summarized. Very few successful practitioners take the time out to tell you, step-by-step, how they do a bankruptcy, or handle a personal injury case, or how to find your way to the courthouse, or any other matter.

They are popular, nevertheless, with experienced lawyers. Many state "continuing education of the bar" associations publish manuals on state law. On a national scale, the American Law Institute-American Bar Association handbooks and those of the Practicing Law Institute are good introductions to unfamiliar areas of the law. See the appendix for a subject listing of national practitioners' manuals.

---

53. The quantity and, in a few cases, the quality of "Law for the Layperson" books have gone up in recent years. They really do attempt to tell you how-to-do-it. Despite their reputation for oversimplification and, sometimes, for error—more than one attorney has taken a secret look at one to get at least a quick sketch of an unfamiliar area.

III. Standard Treatises

The appendix also lists the major national treatises. These works are respected, definitive works on major legal subjects. Most are multivolumed and well supplemented. They enjoy a high reputation as persuasive authority with the courts. Glance at the case of *Executive Jet Aviation, Inc.* vs. *City of Cleveland,* 409 U.S. 249 (1973) and see how often the Supreme Court cites Moore's *Federal Practice,* Gilmore and Black's *Admiralty,* and Benedict's *Admiralty.*

IV. Looseleaf Services

At a minimum, you have now learned that legal research can be time consuming and complex. This is obviously a critical problem for a practicing lawyer. There are few clients willing to fund, at a rate of fifty to a hundred and fifty dollars an hour, extensive sojourns through the labyrinth of a law library.

The documentation in some areas of the law is especially complex. Federal income tax law, for example, is found in the Internal Revenue Code, Treasury Department regulations, Internal Revenue Service rulings, U.S. Tax Court decisions, and U.S. Court of Appeal decisions. These are all separate sets of books with their own peculiar arrangement, indexes, and supplementation. Since most of these sets are government publications, the indexes are frequently inadequate or nonexistent and the supplementation is generally not prompt. Moreover, these are only the primary sources, you still have to search elsewhere for expert commentary, explanation, or summary.

The law book publisher's solution to this problem is the "looseleaf service." Subscribing attorneys seldom have to research beyond the service. A looseleaf service is generally a multivolumed set in three ring or post binders that provides:

(1) The text of all the cases, statutes, regulations, etc. on the topic.

(2) Expert commentary (*i.e.* it serves as a treatise).

(3) A "topical index."

(4) "Finding lists" which enable you to get into the text of the law or the commentary via a citation to a case, statute, or regulation.

(5) Information on new and pending developments (weekly newsletter).

(6) Other special features, *e.g.*
    a. case citators
    b. forms
    c. calendars
    d. glossaries
    e. checklists
(7) Frequent supplementation by means of individual "replacement pages." Typically a subscriber will receive a weekly package of new pages which replace various pages in the service.

Looseleaf services that provide reports of cases serve as a reporter. Recent cases will appear in the looseleaf binders as "advance sheets." At the end of the year, these will cumulate into bound volumes. For example, the Commerce Clearing House, Inc. *Standard Federal Tax Reporter* is accompanied by over one hundred hardbound volumes of *U.S. Tax Cases* and over thirty volumes of *Tax Court Memorandum Decisions*. The text of administrative regulations will also sometimes accompany the service in a series of bound volumes.

Because of the variety of features and arrangements found in looseleaf services, it is not feasible to provide a step-by-step explanation of how to use them. But, each service *has an index*. Start there. Each service also contains its own detailed instructions in a "How to Use" section at the beginning. Simply regard a looseleaf service as a multi-volumed treatise that also contains the text of cases, statutes, and regulations.

Looseleaf services are available on many legal topics, especially those areas that are extensively regulated by administrative agencies.

Correct Citation Form

Hornbooks, Manuals and Treatises:
    W. Prosser, Handbook of the Law of Torts § 96, at 643 (4th ed. 1971)
Looseleaf Services:
    [1982] 3 Stand. Fed. Tax Rep. (CCH) ¶1995

13

American Law Reports (A.L.R.)

A.L.R. is an annotated reporter with indexes and supplements. It is currently in its fourth series. Federal annotations were put in a series of their own in 1969. Illustration 10 charts this.

I. **What Is an "Annotated Reporter"?**

A.L.R. selects cases from throughout the country that are particularly good illustrations of points of law (because of the facts, the opinion, or both). Since it reports the opinions in these cases, it is a reporter.

An annotation follows each opinion. The annotation is a legal essay on the point of law illustrated by the selected case. It gives the background, the issues involved, and summarizes the rules which hold in all jurisdictions with decisions on point. The annotation cites these decisions and arranges them by jurisdiction. In many situations research can begin and end here. Among the thousands of annotations in the various series of A.L.R. there is a good chance you will find one on your point of law.

II. **Indexes and Supplements to A.L.R.**

If you understand what these annotations are and what you can use them for, you should ask yourself what else would such a valuable research tool need. It would need two things: indexes and supplements; which is what all the rest of those red, blue, black, and other colored books on the shelves are. All of them are either providing a way to find the annotation you want or updating an annotation you have already found.

Why are there so many of these indexes and supplements and why do they have so many different names? One thing you can do to bring some order to all this is to realize that each series (A.L.R., 1st–4th, and Federal) has its own set of indexes and supplements. Unfortunately, the names, colors, and form of these indexes and supplements have changed over the sixty plus years that A.L.R. has been published.

Take a look at illustration 10 and we will talk about indexes and supplements.

A. "Indexes:" Digests, Word Indexes, and Quick Indexes

Notice in the chart that *A.L.R.* and *A.L.R. 2d* have three different "indexes." In the earlier days of this publication the editors wanted to give two different ways of finding an annotation: a digest approach and a word index approach. Later they published a "quick index" that combined both approaches.

The digests are an hierarchial arrangement of headnotes under major headings followed by successively narrower subheadings, therefore, you have to analyze your problem first. For example, calling a thief a thief is labeled pleading the truth, which is a defense to an action called slander, which comes under the general area of intentional torts. Few people use the digest approach to *A.L.R.*, so forget about the *Permanent A.L.R. Digest* and the *A.L.R. 2d Digest*.

Next, there are the *A.L.R. Word Index* and *A.L.R. 2d Word Index*. They are like other indexes you have used. You must look under specific factual or legal terms to find a reference to your annotation.

The third type of index is fairly new; it is the *Quick Index*. It includes both specific word entries (like the word indexes) and analytical entries (like the digests). **The *Quick Index* is the only index you should use now.** The "word indexes" for the first and second series are out of date. They will lead you to many superseded annotations. For *A.L.R. Federal* you have a *Quick Index* and a "Tables" volume which gets you into the annotations by means of case names, U.S.C.S., *Statutes at Large*, C.F.R., or other federal citations.

B. Supplements to A.L.R.

After the *Quick Index* has led you to the desired annotation, you need to update it. This means two things: first, you want citations to later cases on the same point; second, you want to discover if your annotation has been revised or superseded. Over the years, as the law changes, the editors write new annotations that supersede older annotations. As you can imagine, most of the annotations in the A.L.R. first series have been replaced in the later series.

On the chart, under "Supplements," you can see that A.L.R. has its *Blue Book, A.L.R. 2d* has its *Later Case Service,* and *A.L.R. 3d, A.L.R. 4th,* and *A.L.R. Federal* have pocket parts. No matter what the form of the supplement, using them is simply a matter of checking through them with your original A.L.R. citation.

Another way of updating is by using the "Annotation History Table" found in the back of the quick index and pocket part for the latest series. This table could save you much time, particularly with a first or second series annotation.

III. Steps in Using A.L.R.

Now, having explained and charted the somewhat complex history and structure of A.L.R., it can be said that, for the third series on the use of A.L.R. is a waltz: you go from the quick index—to the annotation—to the pocket part.

If it is a federal problem, use *A.L.R. Federal;* if not, start with *A.L.R. 3d.* Many of the annotations in the first two series have been superseded and the fourth series is just starting.

Finally, a quick way of updating those first two series, which do not have pocket parts, is to use the "Annotation History Table" in the back of the quick index and pocket part for the latest series.

Don't let A.L.R. intimidate you. Learn to use it. It is a favorite tool of those attorneys who produce above average research in a minimum amount of time.

Correct Citation Form

Annot., 1 A.L.R. 3d 677 (1965)

Illustration 10. *A.L.R.:* An Annotated Reporter
with Indexes and Supplements

Series	Annotated Reports	Indexes			Supplements
First	*A.L.R.* (175 vol.)	*Permanent A.L.R. Digest* (12 vol.)	*A.L.R. Word Index* (4 vol.)	*A.L.R. First Series Quick Index* (1 vol.)	*A.L.R. Blue Book of Supplemental Decisions* (5 vol. + booklet)
Second	*A.L.R. 2d* (100 vol.)	*A.L.R. 2d Digest* (7 vol.)	*A.L.R. Word Index* (3 vol.)	*A.L.R. Second Series Quick Index* (1 vol.)	*A.L.R. 2d Later Case Service* (22 vol. + pocket parts)
Third	*A.L.R. 3d* (100 vol.)	*A.L.R. Quick Index; 3d–4th* (1 vol.)			Pocket parts in each volume of the reports
Fourth	*A.L.R. 4th* (current)	*A.L.R. Quick Index; 3d–4th* (pocket part)			Pocket parts in each volume of the reports
Federal	*A.L.R. Federal* (current)	*Federal Quick Index, Third Edition* (2 vol. + pocket parts)		*A.L.R. Fed; Tables of Cases-Laws- Regs* (1 vol. + pocket part)	Pocket parts in each volume of he reports

14

Encyclopedias

These are easy to use. They all have indexes. You should be familiar with the two national encyclopedias: *American Jurisprudence 2d* (Am. Jur. 2d) and *Corpus Juris Secundum* (C. J. S.). Many states also have an encyclopedia.

A legal encyclopedia synthesizes and arranges the case law within its jurisdictional coverage. If you picked up a volume of *C. J. S.,* you would see that it is a classified arrangement of "black-letter" statements of law (pithy summaries) followed by an overview of general American law on the subject with copious case citations.

Legal encyclopedias have two drawbacks. One, they do not cover statute law as extensively as case law. Two, they often overgeneralize and do not reflect the complexity of changing law. For example, a state encyclopedia would not be a good place to go for a search and seizure problem. However, they often can be valuable as a quick overview in an unfamiliar area of the law and, because of the plentiful citations, as a case finder.

Correct Citation Form

17 C. J. S. Contracts 16, at 615 (1963)
17 Am. Jur. 2d Contracts 171 (1964)

CHAPTER 15

Restatements

I. What Are the Restatements?

The *Restatements of the Law* are products of the highly respected American Law Institute. Founded in 1923, it is an association of judges, law school teachers, and lawyers that promotes uniformity and clarification of laws throughout the United States. Some of its work is in the legislative area, wherein it has produced model codes and statutes. Its primary efforts, however, have been directed towards common law rule making by the courts. For this it has produced its *Restatements of: Agency 2d, Conflict of Laws 2d, Contracts 2d, Foreign Relations, Judgments 2d, Property 2d, Restitution, Security, Torts 2d,* and *Trusts 2d.* Basically, what the A.L.I. does is to survey court decisions from all states on an area of the law, look at the various rules that prevail from state to state, determine what are the preferred rules, then "restate" them in a clear, concise, and organized manner. These restatements are strong persuasive authority in the courts and parts have often been incorporated into a state's common law.

Correct Citation Form

Restatement (Second) of Torts § 565, Comment (1977)

II. Citators for the Restatements

Shepard's publishes a *Restatements of the Law Citations* which gives citations to cases that have cited the *Restatements.*

The American Law Institute publishes a citator/annotator called *Restatement in the Courts.* It gives digests of the cases citing the *Restatements. Restatement in the Courts* has come out in a long series of mostly hardbound supplements through the years. The supplementation is not as current as *Shepard's.*

16

Form Books

I. How They Are Used

A great deal of legal practice includes the drafting of the right piece of paper. There are contracts, pleadings, wills, deeds, leases, applications, and so forth. As soon as you are faced with the necessity for one of these, you may want to see how others have done it. Law firms keep files of their forms, but the largest source of sample forms are found in published "form books." For the most part this chapter will only cover the large multivolume form book sets.

These sets are not the product of experts who have sat down and drafted perfect forms. Rather, they are collections of forms that have actually been used. The publishers generally get them from court records and from the files of law offices. These forms cannot be used verbatim because there never could be a collection large enough to cover all situations. Also, there is no guarantee that they are the best—only that they have been used before.

II. Types of Form Books

Beginners often confuse the different types of form book sets. There are two main types and several special sources of forms.

A. Business Form Books

These are also called "substantive form books" (as opposed to "procedural form books"). This is the most general type of form book. Such sets are usually titled "Legal Forms" by the publisher. They include forms on all types of business contracts, estate planning matters, real estate transactions, and other commercial transactions; everything except court forms.

Business form sets are published for the larger states. The major national sets are:

—*American Jurisprudence Legal Forms 2d*
—*Nichols Cyclopedia of Legal Forms*
—*West's Modern Legal Forms*
—*West's Legal Forms, Second Edition*
—*Rabkin and Johnson's Current Legal Forms with Tax Analysis*

B. Procedural Form Books

This is the other main type of form book set. The terms generally found in the title are: "Pleading," "Practice," or "Procedural." Here you will find any forms that are directed towards a court (pleadings, complaints, answers, motions, petitions, etc.)

Procedural form sets are published for the larger states. The major national sets are:

—*American Jurisprudence Pleading and Practice Forms, Revised.* (Forms for state and federal courts)
—*Bender's Federal Practice Forms*
—*Federal Procedural Forms, Lawyers Edition*
—*West's Federal Forms*

C. Statutory Form Books

Many annotated code sets also contain forms prescribed by statute. Sometimes the publisher will collect these forms into separate volumes and arrange them under the same titles, sections, etc. of the statutes themselves. Other times, the publisher will integrate them into the main set.

D. Special Form Books

Some sets are designed for a special activity, for example: Matthew Bender's *Forms of Discovery* or Bexley's *Oil and Gas Forms.*

E. Practitioners' Manuals

Works that are oriented toward the practitioner will generally have forms. For example, if you were looking for a sample will form, the best place to look might be an estate planning manual for your state.

17

Legal Directories

I. *Martindale-Hubbell*

The preeminent legal directory for well over a hundred years has been the *Martindale-Hubbell Law Directory*. These familiar, thick, annual volumes attempt to list all American and Canadian attorneys. Like all legal directories, it is arranged by state and city. You have to know the city in which the attorney practices. The listings are in two parts in each volume. The first part is called the "Geographical Section" and is a complete listing of names of attorneys and firms. The second "Biographical Section" contains "Informative Professional Cards of Eligible Law Offices."[54]

II. Other Legal Directories

Some jurisdictions (states, counties, cities) will have bar directories. In addition there are many special directories that are sometimes kept current. They include directories of: government officers, legislators, judges and court personnel, attorneys general, legal aid and defender officers, law libraries and librarians, law schools, law teachers, bar associations and other professional societies, lawyer referral offices, out-of-state consulting attorneys, lobbyists, women attorneys, and *Who's Who in American Law.*

---

54. *Martindale-Hubbell* has a number of features in addition to being a directory. The most important of these is the "Law Digests" in the last volume. They are excellent summaries of state and foreign statute law. It is a good place to look for quick answers to uncomplicated questions, especially when you are concerned with the laws of more than one state. For example, it would be easier to survey "legal ages" from state to state by using *Martindale-Hubbell,* than by using each of the individual state annotated codes. If you have a simple question on foreign law and/or do not speak the language, it is also a good source for this.

18

Dictionaries and *Words and Phrases*

The two main legal dictionaries in current use are *Ballentine's Law Dictionary* and *Black's Law Dictionary*. Both provide pronunciations of the more difficult terms and expressions, particularly those in Latin.[55]

Words and Phrases is also a kind of dictionary. If you looked inside you would see that West Publishing Co. made even further use of their case headnotes. They have simply taken the headnotes that dealt with definitions (legal and non-legal) and arranged them under the words and phrases being defined. It can be a very useful and often overlooked case finder when the issue is a definition.

Correct Citation Form for Dictionaries

Black's Law Dictionary 233 (rev. 5th ed. 1979)

---

55. There are two other dictionaries worth noting. *Cochran's Law Lexicon* is a good concise legal dictionary. *Bouvier's Law Dictionary* is a two volume encyclopedia/dictionary that was last published in 1914. *Bouvier's* was noted for its scholarship. It can be useful for the older terms.

Final Matters

Outline

19

Automated Legal Research

I. *LEXIS* and *WESTLAW*

A. Introduction

The growing use of these two marvelous tools is the most exciting and important thing happening in legal research today. But it is beyond the scope of this book to provide an even moderately detailed account of their contents and procedures. Each service has its own manuals, guides, and hands-on training programs. What will be attempted, however, is to give you a general description of the contents of these data bases (aided by illustrations) and a narrative description of a typical kind of search. Hopefully, this armchair experience will better orient you for your first encounter with the terminal and CRT screen.

Incidentally, it was the author's personal experience that once he learned how to sign on he stumbled through the rest of the steps successfully because the screen kept telling him in its own inimitable user-friendly fashion, what his options were and what keys to hit. After doing this a few times, he stumbled less. This is probably the most efficient way for you to learn the basics as well. Of course, you will need further instruction and/or study, to become efficient in using these powerful systems, but the initial self-instruction is relatively easy.

B. General Contents of Data Bases

LEXIS and *WESTLAW* are, perhaps, the most preeminent information retrieval systems anywhere because of:

1. The immensity of their full text document (cases, statutes, regs, etc.) data bases.
2. The accessibility of the documents by any partial citational or textual words or numbers.
3. The easy manipulation of retrieved documents.
4. The user-friendly operating procedures.

Without going into details, we can say that the main data bases include: court reports for the past thirty to fifty years, federal and a few state statutory codes, *Code of Federal Regulations, Federal Register,* attorney general opinions, Presidential documents, U.S. Supreme Court Briefs (*LEXIS*), federal court rules, recent law review articles, a few legal treatises, *Black's Law Dictionary* (*WESTLAW*), *Shepard's,* and other citation services. Illustrations 11 and 12 show some of the actual data base menus from the *LEXIS* and *WESTLAW* screens.

C. Operating Procedures

There are thick manuals describing the contents and operating procedures for *LEXIS* and *WESTLAW,* however, the basic idea is simple and can be summarized into five steps:

(1) Signing on.
(2) Selecting a data base.
(3) Searching through the data base.
(4) Perusing the retrieved documents.
(5) Signing off.

1. Signing on

Sign on procedures vary with the service you are communicating with and the type of terminal you are using. Each subscriber, whether it is an institution or a person, is given a password or ID number, which you enter as part of the sign-on procedure.

2. Selecting a data base

The next step is selecting a data base. Illustrations 11 and 12 show the first three or four screens that come up showing the "menus" of data bases. (*LEXIS* calls them "libraries"; which are further divided into "files"; *WESTLAW* just calls them "data bases").

Page 1 of the *LEXIS* "libraries" (Illustration 11a) lists the General Federal, States, various special subject libraries, law reviews, United Kingdom, French, and European Communities libraries. As you can see, *LEXIS* is used outside the United States. The special subject data bases are used when you know your material will be found in one of those subject areas. It is much faster to search for tax cases in a data base that only contains tax cases. Page 2 of the *LEXIS* "libraries" (Illustration 11b) lists the fifty state and District of Columbia data bases. Illustration 11c shows all the "files" that come under the General Federal (GENFED) library. Look the illustrations over to see the kinds of materials that are in *LEXIS*. Note the dates of coverage. For example, it has all U.S. Supreme Court decisions going back to 1925 in its SUP file.

Page 1 of *WESTLAW* (Illustration 12a) provides you with a directory of their data bases and services. You make your initial selection there and then type in the page number for a fuller description. The illustrations of page 2 through 4 show you some of those fuller descriptions.

Note the various messages on both the *LEXIS* and *WESTLAW* screens that direct you to your next step. You can also type "Help". When all else fails, both systems have toll free numbers for reassuring and helpful human advice.

3. Searching through the data base

Searching a full text data base requires a new kind of skill if you have never done it before. It is not like using an index or using the analytic approach in digests or annotated codes. None of the documents (cases, etc.) in the data bases have been indexed or analyzed. They are simply there full text; so unless you are going to retrieve them by their citations, you have to retrieve them by the words found in the text. Your efficiency as a searcher will depend on how much you know about the language of the law and how it is used in court opinions, statutes, regulations, etc.

For example, let us say that you are looking for U.S. Supreme Court cases on "former jeopardy". After selecting the Supreme Court data base, the machine will ask you for your search terms. If you just enter the phrase "former jeopardy", you will only get the cases in which that exact phrase was used. You will not get cases in which the court used such phrases as "formerly in jeopardy" or "twice placed in jeopardy" or "double jeopardy". You could, of course, get out of this difficulty by just using the word "jeopardy" as your search term. But what about cases in which they did not use "jeopardy", but instead talked about "former acquittal" or "former conviction" or "res judicata"? Do you want those cases too? If so, your search command should read: "jeopardy or acquittal or conviction or res judicata". You will also have to concern yourself with the various forms of the words acquittal and conviction (i.e. acquit, acquitted, acquittal, etc.)

After determining your initial search terms, let us say that the machine tells you that there are 328 cases that used at least one of those terms. You decide that you are only really interested in those former jeopardy cases that dealt with whether two separate acts can constitute the same crime. Now you will have to add an "and" to your original search so that it now reads something like: "jeopardy or acquittal or conviction or res judicata and same crime or identical offense".

Note the use of the conjunctions "and" and "or". *LEXIS* and *WESTLAW* call them "connectors". Choosing connectors is another thing to think about in composing your search. The main other connectors are: "but not" and, in *WESTLAW,* [in] "same sentence", and [in] "same paragraph". Both systems also allow you to use the "W/n" connector. This means "within a certain number of words". For example, "jeopardy" within 10 words of "identical offense" will pull up all the cases in which both expressions are used within ten words of each other.

4. **Perusing the retrieved documents**

Once you have retrieved your cases (or other documents), *LEXIS* and *WESTLAW* give you a number of options for perusing them. You can simply go through page by page, or you can look at only those pages where your search terms appear (*WESTLAW*) or in key-word-in-context fashion in *LEXIS* (i.e. where your search terms appear with a certain number of words on either side) or you can just look at certain segments of the case report, for example, the synopsis segment. If you have retrieved several cases, you can proceed through them one by one or jump forward or backward among them. If your terminal is connected to a printer, you can print all or part of whatever you have retrieved. In most situations, however, you will get your citations and then go into the library to read the reports. You use *LEXIS* and *WESTLAW* mostly as a finding tool. It is not generally convenient to study cases, etc. on CRT's or even from print-outs.

5. **Signing Off**

Completing the simple sign-off procedures is the final step. The computer will compute the time you spent and immediately report it on the screen.

Correct Citation Form for *LEXIS* or *WESTLAW*

Regan v. *Time, Inc.,* No. 82–729 (U.S. Sup. Ct. Jul. 3, 1983) (available July 6, 1984, on *LEXIS,* Genfed library, Sup. file).

Illustrations 11a–11c. Print Outs from *LEXIS* Data Base Menu Screens.

```
Please TRANSMIT the NAME (only one) of the library you want to use.  You may
TRANSMIT the NAME of any library, not only those listed below.  To see a list of
additional libraries, press the NEXT PAGE key.  To see the description of a
particular library, type its page number and then press the TRANSMIT key.
                          LIBRARIES -- PAGE 1 of 2
NAME    PG NAME    PG NAME    PG NAME    PG NAME    PG NAME    PG

- - - - - - U S - L E G A L - - - - - - UK-LEGAL  FR-LEGAL
 GENFED  1            STATES  1           ENGGEN  9 INTNAT 10
                                                   LOIREG 10
 ADMRTY  2 FEDCOM  3 MILTRY  4 LAWREV  5  ENGIND  9 PRIVE  10
 BALDWN  2 FEDSEC  3 PATCOP  4 ABA     5  ENGLG   9 PUBLIC 10
 BANKNG  2 FEDTAX  3 PUBCON  4 CCH     5  EURCOM  9 REVUES 10
 BKRTCY  2 ITRADE  3 TRADE   4           UKIP     9
 DECORP  2 LABOR   3                     UKTAX    9
 ENERGY  2
```

```
LEXIS contains cases decided between the two dates given on the file menus.
Some cases decided before the later date may yet arrive from some courts.

For further explanation, press the H key (for HELP) and then the TRANSMIT key.
```

Illustration 11a. Print out of page 1 from "LIBRARIES" on *LEXIS* screen.
Copyright © 1984 by Mead Data Central. Reprinted with permission.

```
Please TRANSMIT the NAME (only one) of the library you want to use.  You may
TRANSMIT the NAME of any library, not only those listed below.  To see a list of
additional libraries, press the PREV PAGE key.  To see the description of a
particular library, type its page number and then press the TRANSMIT key.
                          LIBRARIES -- PAGE 2 of 2
NAME   PG NAME   PG NAME   PG NAME   PG NAME   PG NAME   PG NAME   PG

 ALA   6 DEL   6 IND   6 MASS  6 NEB   7 NCAR  7 RI    7 VT    7
 ALAS  6 DC    6 IOWA  6 MICH  6 NEV   6 NDAK  7 SCAR  7 VA    8
 ARIZ  6 FLA   6 KAN   6 MINN  6 NH    7 OHIO  7 SDAK  7 WASH  8
 ARK   6 GA    6 KY    6 MISS  7 NJ    7 OKL   7 TENN  7 WVA   8
 CAL   6 HAW   6 LA    6 MO    7 NM    7 ORE   7 TEX   7 WISC  8
 COL   6 IDA   6 MAINE 6 MONT  7 NY    7 PA    7 UTAH  7 WYO   8
 CONN  6 ILL   6 MD    6
```

```
For further explanation, press the H key (for HELP) and then the TRANSMIT key.
```

Illustration 11b. Print out of page 2 from "LIBRARIES" on *LEXIS* screen.
Copyright © 1984 by Mead Data Central. Reprinted with permission.

Please TRANSMIT the abbreviated NAME of the file you want to search. To see a
description of a file, type its page number and press the TRANSMIT key.

```
                               FILES -- PAGE 1 of 1
NAME    PG DESCRIP            NAME    PG DESCRIP       NAME    PG DESCRIP

SUP     1  1/25 - 11/84       CASES   1 All Cases      FEDREG  2  7/1/80-11/20/84*
CIR     1  1/38 - 11/84                                CFR     2  Code of Fed. Regs
FEDCIR  1  10/82 - 11/84      SUPCIR  1 SUP,CIR,FEDCIR ALLREG  2  FEDREG & CFR Files
DIST    1  1/48 - 11/84                                CFR81   2  1981 CFR
CTCL    1  1/60 - 10/84       NEWER   1 Newer Cases    CFR82   2  1982 CFR
                              OLDER   1 Older Cases    CFR83   2  1983 CFR
COMGEN  1  1/60 - 10/84                                CODE    3  U.S. Code
                                                       BRIEFS  3  Sup. Ct. Briefs
FRCP    4  Rules Civ. Pro     RULES   4 All Fed. Rules PRESDC  3  1/20/81 -11/05/84
FRCRP   4  Rules Crim Pro
FRE     4  Rules Evidence
FRAP    4  Rules App. Pro
TAXRUL  4  Rules Tax Ct
CLRUL   4  Rules ClaimsCt
                                                *11/9/84 is
                                                Temporarily Unavailable
```

Illustration 11c. Print out of "GENFED" "FILES—page 1 of 1" on *LEXIS*
screen. Copyright © 1984 by Mead Data Central. Reprinted with
permission.

Illustrations 12a–12d. Print Outs from *WESTLAW* Data Base Menu Screens.

```
                        COPR.  @  WEST 1984 NO CLAIM TO ORIG. U.S. GOVT. WORKS
                          <<<  WESTLAW  DIRECTORY  >>>                     P1
                                    DATABASES
FEDERAL
        GENERAL (statutes, cases, administrative materials) ..........P2
        TOPICAL (tax, securities, labor, etc.) ......................P3
STATE
     MULTISTATE
              GENERAL(includes regional Reporter databases) ...........P4
              TOPICAL(includes texts and periodicals) .................P5
        INDIVIDUAL STATES ...........................................P6
NATIONAL
        GENERAL (includes texts and periodicals) .....................P7
        TOPICAL .....................................................P24
                                  SERVICES
CUSTOMER SERVICE ..................................................P25
TRAINING COURSES ..................................................P26
CASE HIGHLIGHTS ...................................................P27
CCH DATABASES AND SERVICES ........................................P28
DICTIONARIES / WEST DIGEST TOPICS..................................P29
CITATORS
        INSTA-CITE ..................................................P30
        SHEPARD'S ...................................................P31
For information about databases or services, enter page number, e.g., P2
```

Illustration 12a. Print out of "WESTLAW DIRECTORY," "PI". Copyright © 1984 by West Publishing Company. Reprinted with permission.

```
                        COPR.  @  WEST 1984 NO CLAIM TO ORIG. U.S. GOVT. WORKS
                          <<<  FEDERAL GENERAL DATABASES  >>>              P2
            STATUTES                         CASES  continued
USC     U.S. Code ...........P32     U.S.Courts of Appeals, continued
             CASES                   CTA11    Eleventh Circuit ........P62
ALLFEDS    Federal Cases (not        CTADC    D.C. Circuit ............P64
  available to some users) ...P35    CTAF     Federal Circuit .........P66
SCT     U.S. Supreme Court ...P38
CTA     U.S. Courts of               DCT      U.S. District Courts
        Appeals ...........P40                (includes Court of
CTA1    First Circuit ......P42               International Trade) .......P68
CTA2    Second Circuit .....P44      CLCT     U.S. Claims Court .........P71
CTA3    Third Circuit ......P46             ADMINISTRATIVE MATERIALS
CTA4    Fourth Circuit .....P48      CFR      Code of Federal
CTA5    Fifth Circuit ......P50               Regulations ..............P73
CTA6    Sixth Circuit ......P52      FR       Federal Register ..........P75
CTA7    Seventh Circuit ....P54      PRES     Presidential Documents ....P77
CTA8    Eighth Circuit .....P56      CG       Comptroller General .......P78
CTA9    Ninth Circuit ......P58            TEXTS AND PERIODICALS
CTA10   Tenth Circuit ......P60      FTP      Fed. Texts and Periodicals .P79
To access a database, enter its identifier, e.g., USC
For more information about a database enter its page number, e.g., P32
For information about Federal Topical databases, enter P3
```

Illustration 12b. Print out of *WESTLAW* "Federal General Databases," "P2". Copyright © 1984 by West Publishing Company. Reprinted with permission.

```
            COPR.  @  WEST 1984 NO CLAIM TO ORIG. U.S. GOVT. WORKS
            <<<  FEDERAL TOPICAL DATABASES  >>>                   P3

   Scope.  Databases have been developed within selected federal "topical"
areas to aid research.  The following list includes the name of each topical
area, the prefix for the database identifiers within each topic, and the page
number for additional information.

   Admiralty (FADM-___) .........P80      Gov't Operations (FGO-___) ....P124
   Antitrust and                          International Transactions
        Business Reg (FABR-___).P82            (FIT-___) .............P131
   Bankruptcy (FBKR-___) ........P88      Labor (FLB-___) ..............P134
   Communications (FCOM-___) ....P94      National Defense (MJ) ........P141
   Constitution (FCFA-___) ......P99      Patents (FP-___) .............P144
   Copyright (FCP-___) ..........P101     Securities (FSEC-___) ........P149
   Energy (FEN-___) .............P106     Taxation (FTX-___)
   Financial (FFIN-___) .........P111          Comment, Code, Cases ..P161
   Gov't Contracts (FGC-___)                   Admin. Material .......P162
        Code, Cases .........P116     Transportation (FTRAN-___) ....P201
        Admin. Material ......P117
For information about the databases within a topical area, enter the
appropriate page number, e.g., P80
For information about Federal General databases, enter P2
```

Illustration 12c. Print out of *WESTLAW* "Federal Topical Databases," "P3". Copyright © 1984 by West Publishing Company. Reprinted with permission.

```
            COPR.  @  WEST 1984 NO CLAIM TO ORIG. U.S. GOVT. WORKS
            <<<  MULTISTATE GENERAL DATABASES  >>>               P4
   Scope.  "Multistate" databases combine materials from several states.
For information about California cases (formerly CRP; now CA-CS) see P270.
For information about New York cases (formerly NYS; now NY-CS) see P476.

                          CASES
ALLSTATES  All States (and District of Columbia) ......................P204
ATL        Atlantic ..................................................P206
NE         Northeastern ..............................................P209
NW         Northwestern ..............................................P211
PAC        Pacific ...................................................P214
SE         Southeastern ..............................................P218
SO         Southern ..................................................P221
SW         Southwestern ..............................................P223
                  ADMINISTRATIVE MATERIALS
AG         Attorney General Decisions ................................P226
                  TEXTS AND PERIODICALS
MTP        Multistate Texts and Periodicals ..........................P228


To access a database, enter its identifier, e.g., ATL
For more information about a database, enter its page number, e.g., P206
For information about Individual State databases, enter P6
```

Illustration 12d. Print out of *WESTLAW* "Multistate General Databases," "P4". Copyright © 1984 by West Publishing Company. Reprinted with permission.

II. Automated Citation Services

A. *Shepards*

You can Shepardize cases when you are using *LEXIS* or *WEST-LAW*. With *WESTLAW,* if you have a case up on the screen or if you have typed in a case citation, hitting the "Shepardize" key (or typing SH, depending on the kind of terminal) will bring up a typical *Shepard's* display. When you are finished with *Shepard's,* you simply hit the "Go Back" key and you will be back where you were in *WESTLAW.* At the time of this writing, *LEXIS* only permits access by typing in a case citation.

The automated *Shepard's* is updated more promptly than the printed version, but it does not go back as far. It does not, at this time, cover the first series of the Regionals.

B. *INSTA-CITE* and *AUTO-CITE*

Shepard's, of course, gives you every case that has cited your case. *INSTA-CITE* (West Pub. Co.) and *Auto-Cite* (Lawyers Cooperative Pub. Co/Bancroft-Whitney) only cite those cases that *directly* affect the value of your case as precedent. In general this means you get the history of your case (appeals, rehearings, etc.) but not the treatment, unless it is overruled. They also give you fuller citational information on your case, *viz.* exact date of decision, docket number, name of the deciding court and parallel citations. *INSTA-CITE* is accessible through *WEST-LAW* and Auto-Cite through *LEXIS.*

III. *Legal Resources Index*

This is the on-line version of the printed product under the same title. See the *Legal Resources Index* on page 133.

IV. Other Automated Retrieval Systems of Interest to Lawyers

Almost all information currently being published in the United States and many other parts of the world is now accessible via terminals located in libraries and in government and commercial offices. Journal literature, books, monographs, research reports, documents, conference proceedings, directories, and so forth in all fields of the physical and life sciences, social sciences, applied sciences, liberal arts, business, and government is being abstracted and indexed. (Law is one of the very few fields available in full text.)

Many of these fields could be of obvious interest to the legal profession. For example, you can get access to:

—All Congressional hearings, reports, debates, and other documents.
—Legislative developments from all fifty states.
—The contents of the *Federal Register.*
—All federal statistical publications.
—Government contract award announcements.
—The records of companies filing reports to the SEC.
—Financial market information from Dow Jones.
—The contents of the *Wall Street Journal,* the *New York Times,* and other large newspapers.
—Information on foundations and grant awards.
—Information on world population, energy, ecology, poverty, etc.

V. Why Isn't All Legal Research Automated?

Automation has come to legal research on a significant scale only within the past few years and, for the most part, only in the case finding area. On the surface it might appear that this complex, time consuming, and somewhat mechanical task is ripe for extensive automation.

It has not happened sooner and more pervasively, however, for a number of reasons. First, the traditional printed sources are fairly efficient. As was noted previously, publishers have been ingenious in keeping American law accessible. Looseleaf services, for example, compete fairly well with the computer. If you can afford the subscription price, within a week, you can get the text of new laws, fully indexed, and completely integrated into your service. Another reason that the computer has not supplanted the books is that the latter are a superior vehicle for text. The text of a court decision, for example, is more readable, portable, permanent, and randomly accessible (flipping pages) in a book than on a cathode ray tube or computer printout. In general, one can say that books are superior for holding text while automation is superior for indexing and searching text. *Lexis* and *Westlaw* are better than a digest for finding cases. Still another reason is that it has not become popular for searching statutes. The only state statutory data bases are New York and Ohio (*LEXIS* only). The reasons for this may be that the printed annotated statutes are fairly efficient tools and, secondly, a computer is entirely literal in its "thinking" and there are too many variations in statutory citation. For example, is it N.J. Rev. Stat. §14A:5-2; or 14 A: 5-2; or Title 14A Chapter 5, section 2; or N.J. Stat. Anno . . . ? There is almost a limitless number of combinations of letters, numbers, spaces, and symbols for a statutory citation that judges might use in their opinions. Naturally, the computer reads each space, each mark of punctuation, etc. Finally, automated legal information retrieval has not supplanted traditional methods because it is expensive. Published law, particularly court decisions, comprises a huge body of text that must be translated into machine readable form. It must be absolutely accurate and supplemented daily. Only the larger law firms and agencies can currently afford *Lexis* or *Westlaw*. Costs are in a range of a full time attorney's salary.

20

Research Strategy

I. Adopt a Plan.

Your research will be more fruitful and efficient if you start with a plan, even if it gets modified as it goes along. Make deliberate steps from one source to another. Do not let the footnotes and citations chase you all over the library until your head is spinning and you cannot remember where you started and why you are where you are.

Unfortunately, despite all the "how-to-do-it" articles and books on the subject, there is no single way to proceed on every research problem. It is one thing to provide the steps in using *Shepard's,* and another to flow chart a model plan for all research projects. There are too many variables, including: the sophistication of the researcher, the time available, the kinds of books available, the importance of the project, and so on.

II. Know Your Options.

Knowing your options means having a fundamental knowledge of law books. A fundamental knowledge does not mean a mastery of the details. It simply means knowing the major types of law books, what they primarily contain, and the rudimentary steps for getting into their contents. In the author's experience, those who fail at legal research are not those who do not know that ". . . a parallel conversion table in volume 21 of the First Decennial translates from the Century section numbers to the Decennial Key Numbers." Those who fail are those who cannot find the regulations of the U.S. Equal Employment Opportunity Commission, county court rules, or the text of a recent state statute.[56]

---

56. Lawyers have suffered malpractice judgments because they did not take their legal research seriously. See *Smith* v. *Lewis,* 13 Cal.3d 349, 118 Cal. Rptr. 621, 530 P.2d 589 (1975). See generally Annot., 45 A.L.R.2d 5,15–17.

To explain this principle more graphically—you should be able to stand in the lobby of a law library with your research problem and be able to picture in your mind the basic organizational structure of all those law books: annotated codes with legislative services; legislative history documents; reporters, digests, and *Shepard's;* administrative registers and codes; law reviews and their indexes; A.L.R.; looseleaf services; practitioners manuals; treatises; pleading and practice sets; form books; records and briefs; dictionaries; directories. After an almost unconscious mental review of these tools, you can then devise a rational strategy or at least know where to start.

Look over the "Outline of American Law Books" on page 172 et seq. If all those titles, book descriptions, and interrelationships are meaningful to you, you have a good foundation in legal research. If you can compose essentially the same outline on your own, you are a competent legal researcher.

III. Make Adequate Notes at Each Step in Your Research.

A typical scenario of a beginner, particularly a first year law student researching for a moot court brief goes as follows: First, days are spent finding dozens of cases and statutes, some law review articles, maybe an A.L.R. annotation, and possibly something from C.F.R., or other sources. Then slips of paper are dutifully inserted into each volume at the appropriate page. The volumes are then lined up at the table or carrel. Finally, he or she sits back and surveys this regiment of law books, with markers bristling from the top, and the disheartening realization dawns that there has been no progress. There is nothing that can be done with all those closed books.

Something can be done, however, with notes that have been made on index cards or separate sheets of paper.

Whatever format you use, the general way to proceed is: *for every item you encounter that might be useful, take complete notes immediately.* Brief the cases, copy quotes from statutes and secondary sources, and use the photocopier. Write down the complete citation while you have it. Each case, each statute, etc. goes on a separate card or sheet. Do not scratch down on a tablet some hurried sentences and partial citations, expecting to return to the source later. Coming back later wastes time and, besides, once those scratchy notes pile up, there will not be much you can do with them.

After you have found all your possible sources and reduced them to briefs, quotes, or ideas on separate cards or sheets, you then have something that you can manipulate both mentally and physically. You can now reread these items and start forming your lines of argument. Once you determine the outline of your argument (or defense or exposition), you can arrange your cards or sheets according to that outline, throw out those you are not going to use, maybe clean up a few odds and ends of research, and start writing your brief. Most of your thinking and writing will have already been done.

IV. Research in Solo Practice: Stopping the Bleeding and Major Surgery

In a law office you basically need a library to meet two research situations: one, stopping the bleeding and two, performing major surgery. Most of what has been covered in this manual deals with major surgery, *i.e.* in-depth research to advise a client, argue a motion, prepare for a trial, handle an appeal, and so on. But sometimes a client needs first aid. He or she needs to get out of jail, or respond to a summons, or simply get some quick counsel to relieve anxiety. For this kind of situation you need a few, familiar, trusted sources close at hand. At a minimum, they should include a pleading and practice set with forms, some continuing education of the bar or other practitioners manuals on the areas of the law you are liable to encounter, and, if your state is lucky enough to have a good one, an encyclopedia or other summary treatment of all state law. After you have made a few dollars, your next purchase should be your state's annotated codes. When you have major surgery, use the nearest county, bar, or law school library.

Aside from law books, subscribe to all the local newspapers and as many of the top national newspapers as you can (*New York Times* and *Washington Post* especially). Newspapers report on the stuff of which litigation is made. They will prepare you for the clients that come in and for what is coming in the law. Newspapers thrive on the controversies, the conflicts, the social changes, and the bad news that prompts people to walk into your office. Are day care centers springing up in the residential areas of your town? Is the planning commission considering an annexation? Has the city council raised business license fees? Is the grand jury investigating unsanitary conditions in the county jail? Is there a bill in the state legislature to liberalize abortion? Is the Immigration and Naturalization Service cracking down on illegal aliens? Is the I.R.S. looking more closely at business expense deductions? Lawyers are avid readers of newspapers.

V. Some Other Hints and Notes on Research Strategy

1. When you are in an unfamiliar area of the law, go to the commentaries:

   —Law review articles are especially good for new areas of the law.

   —A.L.R. is great for persuasive authority.

   —Get familiar with your state's practitioners manuals and encyclopedia.

   —If there is a looseleaf service on the topic, it has everything.

2. Find the statutes first, then the cases and the regulations.

3. Any lawyer worth his or her salt can find ambiguity in statutory language. Look for a legislative history argument.

4. Constitutions and court rules can be found in the annotated codes.

5. Do not forget records and briefs. Pick someone's brain.

6. Use *U.S. Law Week* for all recent Supreme Court cases and many recent state and federal cases of note.

7. Local legal newspapers are often the first source to report opinions.

8. *Restatements* are excellent persuasive authority.

9. Uniform laws are all collected in a set called *Uniform Laws Annotated* (U.L.A.)

10. Parallel citations can be found in *Shepard's* or the *Blue and White Books*

11. There is a *Shepard's* for every reporter.

12. When you only have the name of a case, go to a table of cases in a digest for the full citation. Digest tables of cases are updated in the advance sheets.

13. Popular name? Use *Shepard's Acts and Cases by Popular Name.*

14. Cannot figure out a citation abbreviation? Use Powers, *The Legal Citation Directory;* or the appendix in Price, *Effective Legal Research. Shepard's* uses its own abbreviations—look in front.

15. Be conscious of jurisdiction. Illinois courts are ten times more interested in Illinois cases than those of any other state.

16. There are national and state form books. The two major types are business form books and court form books.

17. Want to find the best text on a certain topic? Ask an experienced law librarian.

Illustration 13. Outline of American Law Books.

CASES

Reporters

(federal)	(state)
United States Reports	West's Regional Reporters
Supreme Court Reporter	Official reporters for some states
U.S. Supreme Court Reports, Lawyers Ed.	
U.S. Law Week	
Federal Reporter	
Federal Supplement	

LEXIS and *WESTLAW*

Shepard's (Cases editions)

Case Finders

Digests: State, Regional, Decennial, Federal and U.S. Supreme Court

LEXIS and *WESTLAW*

Commentaries (*q.v.* on this chart)

Records and Briefs

CODES

Constitutions

Found in the federal and state annotated codes.

Session Laws

(state)
"Statutes", "Laws", "Public and Local Acts", "Session Laws", "Acts and Resolves", "General and Special Laws", etc.

(federal)
Statutes at Large

Annotated Codes

(state)
"Code", "Revised Code", "Annotated Code", "Revised Statutes", "General Statutes", "Consolidated Statutes", "Laws", etc.

(federal)
United States Code Annotated (U.S.C.A.)
United States Code Service (U.S.C.S.)

Shepard's (Statutes editions)

Uniform Laws Annotated

Legislative History
(federal)

U.S. Code: Congressional and Administrative News
CCH Congressional Index
Congressional Information Service

Local Codes

City charters and city and county codes of ordinances

CODES *(Continued)*

Administrative Codes

(federal)

(state)

Most states have an administrative register and/or code

Federal Register
Code of Federal Regulations (C.F.R.)
Shepard's C.F.R. Citations
LEXIS and *WESTLAW*

Court Rules
(Legislative)

(Judicial)

In federal and state annotated codes under: "Civil Procedure", "Criminal Procedure", "Evidence", "Courts", "Practice", "Judiciary", "Probate", "Family Law", etc.

For Entire
Jurisdiction

In federal and state annotated codes under: "Rules", "Rules of Court", "Civil and Criminal Rules", "Appellate Rules", "Supreme Court Rules", "Municipal Court Rules", "Magistrate Court Rules", *etc.*

Local Court
Rules

Clerk of the court's office, pleading and practice sets and other commercial publications of local rules.

Treaties

Statutes at Large (until 1950)
U.S. Treaties and Other International Agreements (1950–)
Treaties in Force
Shepard's United States Citations (Statutes edition)

COMMENTARIES

Periodicals

Index to Legal Periodicals
Current Law Index (1980–) (Also an on-line version)
Legal Resources Index (microfilm)
Shepard's Law Review Citations

Hornbooks, Manuals, Treatises and Looseleaf Services

(See Appendix for list of titles by subject)

American Law Reports

Encyclopedias

(national)   (state)
Corpus Juris Secundum   Many states have their own encyclopedias
American Jurisprudence 2nd

Restatements

Agency, Conflict of Laws, Contracts, Property, Torts, and Trusts, etc.
Shepard's Restatements of the Law Citations

Form Books

Business Form Books
Procedural Form Books   See Appendix for titles
Practitioners' Manuals

Martindale-Hubbel Law Directory

Dictionaries

Ballentine's Law Dictionary
Black's Law Dictionary
Words and Phrases

Appendix: Selected National Commentaries

Selected National Treatises, Practitioners' Manuals, Restatements, and Looseleaf Services are arranged under the following subjects:

Administrative Law
Admiralty
Agency
Antitrust and Trade Regulation
Arbitration
Associations
Automobile
Aviation
Banks and Banking
Commercial Law
Community Property
Conflict of Laws
Constitutional Law
Contracts
Copyright
Corporations and Partnerships
Criminal Law and Procedure
Debtor and Creditor
Domestic Relations
Energy and Public Utilities
Environment
Estates and Estate Planning
Evidence
Food, Drugs, and Cosmetics
Form Books—Business
Form Books—Procedural

Government Contracts
Immigration Law
Insurance
International Law
Labor
Malpractice
Mining
Municipal Corporations
Oil and Gas
Patents
Practice and Procedure—Federal
Practice and Procedure—General
Property, Real and Personal
Restitution
Securities
Statutory Construction
Taxation
Torts
Trademarks and Unfair Competition
Water
Workmen's Compensation
Zoning and Land Planning

Administrative Law

Cooper. *State Administrative Law.*
Davis. *Administrative Law Treatise.*
Mezines, Stein, and Gruff. *Administrative Law.*
Pike and Fischer. *Administrative Law.*

Admiralty

Arzt. *Marine Laws.*
Benedict. *Admiralty.*
Gilmore. *The Law of Admiralty.*
Knauth. *American Law of Ocean Bills of Lading.*
Norris. *The Law of Seamen.*
Norris. *Maritime Personal Injuries.*

Agency

ALI. *Restatement of the Law, Second, Agency.*
Reuschlein. *Handbook on the Law of Agency and Partnership.*
Sell on Agency.

Antitrust and Trade Regulation (see also Food, Drugs, and Cosmetics)

Areeda and Turner. *Antitrust Law.*
BNA. *Antitrust and Trade Regulation Report.*
CCH. *Trade Regulation Reporter.*
von Kalinowski. *Antitrust Laws and Trade Regulation.*
Kanwit. *Federal Trade Commission.*
Kintner. *A Robinson-Patman Primer.*
Kintner. *Federal Anti-Trust.*
Kintner. *Primer on the Law of Mergers.*
Reams and Ferguson. *Federal Consumer Protection.*
Rothschild and Carroll. *Consumer Protection Reporting Service.*
Stickells. *Federal Control of Business.*
Toulmin. *Anti-Trust Laws*

Arbitration

Domke on Commercial Arbitration.

Associations

Webster. *The Law of Associations.*

Automobile

Blashfield. *Automobile Law and Practice.*

Aviation

Kreindler. *Aviation Accident Law.*
Speiser and Kraus. *Aviation Tort Law.*

Banks and Banking

CCH. *Federal Banking Law Reporter.*

Commercial Law (See also Debtor and Creditor)

Anderson. *Uniform Commercial Code.*
Bender's Uniform Commercial Code Service.
CCH. *Consumer Credit Guide and Secured Transactions Guide.*
Callaghan & Co. *Uniform Commercial Code Reporting Service.*
Gilmore. *Security Interests in Personal Property.*
Squillante. *The Law of Modern Commercial Practices.*
Williston. *Sales.*

Community Property

McClanahan. *Community Property Law in the United States.*

Conflict of Laws

ALI. *Restatement of the Law, Second, Conflict of Laws.*
Leflar. *American Conflicts Law.*
Weintraub. *Commentary on the Conflict of Laws.*

Constitutional Law

Antieau. *Modern Constitutional Law.*
Nowak, Rotunda, and Young. *Constitutional Law.*
Tribe. *American Constitutional Law.*
U.S. Government Printing Office. *The Constitution of the United States of America Annotated.*

Contracts

ALI. *Restatement of the Law, Second, Contracts.*
Corbin on Contracts.
Williston. *Treatise on the Law of Contracts.*

Copyright

Lindey. *Entertainment, Publishing and the Arts.*
Nimmer on Copyright.

Corporations and Partnerships

CCH. *Corporation Law Guide.*
Fletcher. *Cyclopedia of the Law of Private Corporations.*
McKnight. *The Complete Partnership Manual and Guide.*
Matthew Bender and Co. *Business Organizations, with Tax Planning.*
Oleck. *Non-Profit Corporations.*
O'Neal. *Close Corporations.*

Criminal Law and Procedure

BNA. *Criminal Law Reporter.*
Bailey and Rothblatt. (Various titles)
La Fave. *Search and Seizure.*
Matthew Bender and Co. *Business Crime.*
Matthew Bender and Co. *Criminal Defense Techniques.*
Orfield. *Criminal Procedure under the Federal Rules.*
Perkins. *Criminal Law.*
Torcia. *Wharton's Criminal Evidence.*
Torcia. *Wharton's Criminal Law.*
Torcia. *Wharton's Criminal Procedure.*

Debtor and Creditor (See also Commercial Law)

CCH. *Bankruptcy Law Reporter.*
CCH. *Consumer Credit Guide.*
CCH. *Secured Transactions Guide.*
Collier on Bankruptcy.
Cowans. *Bankruptcy Law and Practice.*
Fonseca. *Handling Consumer Credit Cases.*
Lawyers Co-op. Bankruptcy Service.
Matthew Bender and Co. *Debtor-Creditor Law.*

Domestic Relations

BNA. *Family Law Reporter.*
Baxter. *Marital Property.*
Lindey. *Separation Agreements and Ante-Nuptial Contracts.*
Matthew Bender and Co. *Child Custody and Visitation.*

Energy and Public Utilities (See also Mining; Oil and Gas; and Water)

CCH. *Energy Management.*
CCH. *Nuclear Regulation Reports.*
Matthew Bender and Co. *Federal Power Service.*
Public Utilities Reports.

Environment

> BNA. *Environment Reporter.*
> CCH. *Pollution Control Guide.*
> Environmental Law Institute. *Environmental Law Reporter.*
> Grad. *Treatise on Environmental Law.*
> Yannacone and Cohen. *Environmental Rights and Remedies.*

Estates and Estate Planning (See also Community Property)

> ALI. *Restatement of the Law, Second, Trusts.*
> Bergin and Haskell. *Preface to Estates in Land and Future Interests.*
> Bogert. *Trusts and Trustees.*
> Casner. *Estate Planning.*
> Murphy. *Will Clauses.*
> Nossaman. *Trust Administration and Taxation.*
> *Page on the Law of Wills.*
> Prentice Hall. *Estate Planning.*
> Research Institute of America. *Estate Planning and Taxation Coordinator.*
> Scott. *The Law of Trusts.*
> Simes and Smith. *The Law of Future Interests.*
> University of Miami Law Center. *Institute on Estate Planning.*

Evidence

> Callaghan and Co. *Federal Rules of Evidence Service.*
> *Jones on Evidence, Civil and Criminal.*
> Louisell and Mueller. *Federal Evidence.*
> Weinstein's Evidence. (Federal)
> Wigmore. *Evidence.*

Food, Drugs, and Cosmetics

> CCH. *Food, Drug, Cosmetic Law Reporter.*
> O'Reilly. *Food and Drug Administration.*

Form Books—Business (See also individual subjects)

> *Am Jur Legal Forms.*
> *Nichols Cyclopedia of Legal Forms.*
> Rabkin and Johnson. *Current Legal Forms.*
> Warren. *Forms of Agreements.*
> West. *Modern Legal Forms.*
> West. *Legal Forms.*

Form Books—Procedural (See also Practice and Procedure)

American Jurisprudence Pleading and Practice Forms. (State and Federal)
Bender's Federal Practice Forms.
Bender's Forms of Discovery.
Federal Procedural Forms, Lawyers Edition.
West's Federal Forms.

Government Contracts

CCH. *Government Contracts Reporter.*

Immigration Law

Gordon and Rosenfield. *Immigration Law and Procedure.*
National Lawyers Guild. *Immigration Law and Defense.*

Insurance

Anderson. *Couch on Insurance.*
Appleman. *Insurance Law and Practice.*
CCH. *Automobile Insurance Law Reports.*
CCH. *Fire and Casualty Insurance Law Reports.*
CCH. *Life-Health and Accident Insurance Law Reports.*
Long. *The Law of Liability Insurance.*
Magarick. *Successful Handling of Casualty Claims.*
Schermer. *Automobile Liability Insurance.*
Woodroof. *Automobile Insurance and No-Fault.*

International Law

ALI. *Restatement of the Law, Second, Foreign Relations Law of the United States.*
Kaye, *et al. International Trade Practice.*
Lowenfeld. *International Economic Law.*
Streng. *International Business Planning: Law and Taxation.*
Von Glahn. *Law Among Nations.*

Labor

BNA. *Labor Relations Reporter.*
CCH. *Labor Law Reporter.*
Research Institute of America. *Federal Regulation of Employment Service.*

Malpractice

Ficarra. *Surgical and Allied Malpractice.*
Louisell and Williams. *Medical Malpractice.*
Mallen and Levit. *Legal Malpractice.*
Stern. *A Practical Guide to Preventing Legal Malpractice.*

Mining

Rocky Mountain Mineral Law Foundation. *American Law of Mining.*

Municipal Corporations

Antieau. *Municipal Corporation Law.*
McQuillin. *Law of Municipal Corporations.*

Oil and Gas

Kuntz. *Law of Oil and Gas.*
Summers. *Oil and Gas.*
Williams and Meyers. *Oil and Gas Law.*

Patents

Deller's Walker on Patents.
Eckstrom. *Licensing in Foreign and Domestic Operations.*
Horwitz. *Patent Office Rules and Practice.*
Matthew Bender and Co. *Patent Law and Practice Series.*

Practice and Procedure—Federal

Callaghan and Co. *Cyclopedia of Federal Procedure.*
Callaghan and Co. *Federal Rules Service and Digest.*
Devitt. *Federal Jury Practice and Instructions.*
Lawyers Co-op Co. *Federal Procedure.*
Moore's Federal Practice.
Stern and Gressman. *Supreme Court Practice.*
Volz. *West's Federal Practice Manual.*
Wright and Miller. *Federal Practice and Procedure.*

Practice and Procedure—General

ALI. *Restatement of the Law, Second, Judgments.*
Am Jur Proof of Facts.
Am Jur Trials.
Belli. *Modern Trials.*
Danner. *Pattern Interrogatories.*
Dobbs on Remedies.
Goldstein. *Trial Technique.*

Newberg on Class Actions.
Reid's Branson Instructions to Juries.
Schweitzer. *Cyclopedia of Trial Practice.*

Property, Real and Personal (See also Community Property; Estates and Estate Planning)

ALI. *Restatement of the Law, Second, Property.*
American Law of Property. (Little, Brown and Co.)
Basye. *Clearing Land Titles.*
Brown on Personal Property.
Friedman. *Leases.*
Kratovil. *Modern Mortgage Law and Practice.*
Kratovil. *Modern Real Estate Documentation.*
Kratovil. *Real Estate Law.*
Matthew Bender and Co. *Real Estate Transactions Series.*
McMichael. *Leases, Percentage, Short and Long Term.*
Osborne, Nelson, and Whitman. *Real Estate Finance Law.*
Powell on Real Property.
Reskin and Sakai. *Modern Real Estate and Mortgage Forms; Condominiums.*
Thompson on Real Property.
Tiffany. *Real Property.*

Restitution

ALI. *Restatement of Restitution.*
Palmer. *Law of Restitution.*

Securities

Bines. *Law of Investment Management.*
CCH. *Blue Sky Law Reporter.*
CCH. *Federal Securities Law Reporter.*
Clark Boardman Co. *Securities Law Series.*
Jaffe. *Brokers-Dealers and Securities Markets.*
Loss. *Securities Regulation.*
Prentice Hall. *Securities Regulation.*

Statutory Construction

Sutherland. *Statutes and Statutory Construction.*

Taxation

BNA. *Tax Management.*
CCH. *Inheritance, Estate, and Gift Tax Reports.*
CCH. *Standard Federal Tax Reports.*
Mertens. *Law of Federal Income Taxation.*

Prentice Hall. *Federal Taxes.*
Rabkin and Johnson. *Federal Income, Gift, and Estate Taxation.*
Research Institute of America, Inc. *Federal Tax Coordinator.*
Stephens, Maxfield and Lind. *Federal Estate and Gift Taxation.*

Torts (See also Automobile; Aviation; Food, Drugs, and Cosmetics; and Malpractice)

ALI. *Restatement of the Law, Second, Torts.*
Allen Smith Co. *Lawyer's Medical Cyclopedia.*
BNA. *Product Safety and Liability Reporter.*
CCH. *Products Liability Reporter.*
Dixon. *Drug Product Liability.*
Dooley. *Modern Tort Law.*
Frumer and Friedman. *Products Liability.*
Gordy, Gray *et al. Attorneys' Textbook of Medicine.*
Harper and James. *Law of Torts.*
Houts. *Lawyers' Guide to Medical Proof.*
Hursch and Bailey. *American Law of Products Liability.*
Kelner. *Personal Injury.*
Matthew Bender and Co. *Courtroom Medicine Series.*
Matthew Bender and Co. *Damages in Tort Actions.*
Matthew Bender and Co. *Personal Injury Series.*
Prosser. *Handbook of the Law of Torts.*
Speiser. *The American Law of Torts.*
Speiser. *Recovery for Wrongful Death.*

Trademarks and Unfair Competition

Callmann. *Unfair Competition, Trademarks, and Monopolies.*
Gilson. *Trademark Protection and Practice.*
McCarthy. *Trademarks and Unfair Competition.*

Water

Water and Water Rights. (Allen Smith Co. Pub.)

Workmen's Compensation

Larson. *Workmen's Compensation Law.*

Zoning and Land Planning

Anderson. *American Law of Zoning.*
BNA. *Housing and Development Reporter.*
Nichols on Eminent Domain.
Rohan. *Zoning and Land Use Controls.*
Williams. *American Land Planning Law.*
Yokley. *Zoning Law and Practice.*

Index